Harry Potter Smart Talk

The Leaky Cauldron's Potter Pundits Explore the Literary Depths, Heights, and Humor of J. K. Rowling's Hogwarts Saga

Foreword by Melissa Anelli, Author of 'Harry, A History'

James Thomas, Travis Prinzi, and John Granger (editor)

For information, contact Unlocking Press
www.UnlockingPress.com

Unlocking Press titles may be purchased for business or promotional use or special sales.

Cover Design by Joyce Odell
10 - 9 - 8 - 7 - 6 - 5 - 4 - 3 - 2 - 1

ᴜnlocking
press
www.UnlockingPress.com

ISBN 978-0-9829633-0-2

Table of Contents

FOREWORD

•

The Ivory Tower
Inside Hagrid's Hut

Melissa Anelli
'Harry, A History' Author, Leaky Cauldron
Webmistress, and PotterCast Hostess
Explains Why She Loves the Potter Pundits

I AM A BIT of a Johnny-come-lately to the world of *Harry Potter* academia. Not having the doctorate degree I thought it required to participate in that sect of the phenomenon, I treated it like my (or perhaps Ron Weasley's) least-talked-about cousin. My usual *Harry Potter* experience lies in the more mainstream, pop culture-based world of Web sites, podcasts and films. One of the reasons *Harry* works so well, I believe, is because it stirs emotions and reactions that aren't exclusive to those who have done fellowships at Oxford University. So why would I need to hear someone's polysyllabic discussion about 20th century modifications to the post-modernist spiritual belief structure in neo-classical feminist renditions of children's lit?

The answer is that I don't, and neither should you. (And in the very exaggerated instance above me, neither should anyone.)

My mistake, and the mistake of so many before me, was to believe that *Harry Potter* and academia could only coexist inside a stuffy ivory tower. I knew J.K. Rowling had not drawn her immense magical world and characters without reference (she frequently talks about how her classical education informed the books) but did not for a moment imagine how digging for the sources of these inspirations might broaden and deepen my understanding of the method behind the magic. I, like many *Harry Potter* fans, always enjoyed occasionally rifling through historical sources, myths and legends to discover connections. As just one example, the series' only phoenix, a bird that occasionally erupts into colorful flame and is reborn from the ashes, takes his name from Guy Fawkes, a revolutionary in whose honor Bonfire Night is celebrated; the day I read this I felt like I had unlocked a special secret that had been laid in the books for only me to find. Few dedicated *Harry Potter* fans go their entire fandom without digging up a couple of these gems, but we also tend to treat them as though they are sprinkled through, and not revelatory of, the story.

Cue the Potter Pundits, who came to the Leaky and PotterCast staff in 2009, wondering if there was a way to merge a more serious discussion of *Harry*'s literary merits to our more populist program. We'd all been to their talks at conferences and been transfixed at the easy way they married the results of serious intellectual research and light browsing through the *Harry Potter* books, inviting deeper study of the texts while making doing so sound as fun as it had been to read them the first time around. It was as though that same ivory tower had been – to use a favorite academic word – deconstructed and rebuilt as Hagrid's hut. We were thrilled to bring them onto our show, where they have brought the same ideas to the tens of thousands of people who listen weekly, and celebrate the space in the *Harry Potter* fandom where academia is not anathema to passion and fun.

Do I always agree with everything the Pundits conclude about the *Harry Potter* books? No, and that's something I think the three Pundits themselves would call a triumph. The idea of their punditry isn't to present a pretty, packaged answer to every riddle, or the definitive origin of every idea that exists in *Harry Potter*. No one wants you to accept any one person's interpretation wholecloth. The idea, and the idea of this book, is to open that conversation, to get more people thinking about the themes, symbology and origins, and how these things are presented, so that the *Harry Potter* books become even more precious than they were before you tried.

I know they are to me.

-Melissa Anelli
September 2010

What is a Potter Pundit?

An Introduction to 'Harry Potter Smart Talk'

YOU ARE A POTTER Pundit! A Potter Pundit is a "serious reader," by which I don't mean a swotty snob that cannot enjoy anything written in the last thirty years. A "serious reader" is one that not only reads a good book more than once but also wants to know more about it – a lot more about it!

- How does this novel work its magic?
- What does it owe the books that came before it?
- Why am I always surprised at the end?

And, most important…
- *"What does it mean?"*

Joanne Rowling's Hogwarts Saga has inspired millions of readers to become 'Potter Pundits' and a lot of them listen to the informative and entertaining PotterCasts on the Leaky Cauldron web site. In 2009 at the LeakyCon in Boston and Azkatraz in San Francisco, the PotterCast hosts -- Melissa Anelli, John Noe, and Frankie Franco III – met with John Granger and Travis Prinzi to discuss recording segments of fun and friendly literary discussion to supplement all they do reporting global Potter news. We quickly came to an agreement and have been having fun talking about Harry ever since!

Fortunately, Pundits listening to these segments seemed to enjoy them, too. By year's end, with the addition of Pepperdine professor James Thomas, the three Potter Pundits had won the *Leaky Award* for "Favorite Leaky Moment in *2009*" as voted on by fandom.

When we realized all three Pundits were speaking at the HPEF Infinitus 2010 fan convention in Orlando, I decided (that would be 'John') that we should put together a 'Greatest Hits' collection of the best Pundit segments from PotterCast along with excerpts from books we're writing and talks we've given as a sampler for PotterCast fans and listeners. My wife typed up four transcripts which I edited for intelligibility and then each Pundit put together two papers from books-in-progress, talk files, or projects that we were most excited about. This "Potter Pundits Greatest Hits" collection, then, is the cutting edge of what we talk about, not only on air at PotterCast but when we get together, as well as a bit of what we have done on at The Leaky Cauldron. We look forward to seeing you in Orlando for Leaky Con 2011 to talk with you about these ideas!

Time for the thank you's before the curtain closes…

I'd like to thank Joyce Odell for her cover, design, my wife Mary for typing up the transcripts, Paul, Christina, David, and Toni for their enthusiasm about the Pundits idea at LeakyCon, Lev Grossman for his kind words, Amy H. Sturgis for joining us to talk about Gothic literature, Travis Prinzi for making the Pundit PotterCast segments possible through his technical wizardry, and to James Thomas for the dry humor, sobriety, and Malibu perspective that make the programs fun.

Thank you most of all to Melissa, John, and Frak for welcoming three nerds into fandom's best podcast and fan site, The Leaky Cauldron – and thank you PotterCast listeners, the real Potter Pundits, for tuning in, for the great feedback and requests for shows you have sent in, and for the fun James, Thomas, and I get to have as Leaky's semi-official Geek Squad.

Harry Potter Rules!

Gratefully,

John Granger

John Granger
john@HogwartsProfessor.com

PART 1: CHAPTER 1

Luna Lovegood

Why We Love the Ravenclaw Moon Shot

TRAVIS PRINZI: HELLO, AND welcome to another segment of the Potter Pundits. We listened to your requests, and we wanted to go back to that original ... and explained that we wanted to hear your requests. You all said that you wanted to talk about characters. And I think the most popular requests were Luna and one of the Weasleys. We put it to a vote and we are going to do something on Luna.

Our Pundits are here. We have John Granger, author of *The Deathly Hallows Lectures*, and his upcoming book on the Twilight series, *Spotlight*. Welcome, John.

John: Great to be here, Travis, as always.

Travis: And James Thomas, author of *Repotting Harry Potter*, is also with us. Hi, James.

James: Hi, how are you, Travis?

Travis: I'm doing well, and of course I'm Travis Prinzi, author of *Harry Potter and Imagination* and we are here to talk about Luna Lovegood, one of the most loved characters, who I think for many readers didn't get enough page time for plotting reasons, but let's begin with what page time she got. Let's talk about you guys' favorite scenes. What are your favorite Luna moments in the series?

John: For me it's the Ravenclaw door in *Deathly Hallows*. When Harry is dispatched to find the diadem that has no measure, etc., and he can't get past this door. He arrives at the Ravenclaw door and there's no pink lady there, he has to actually figure something out, and the door asks him which came first, the Phoenix or the Flame. This is a chicken and the egg question from the magical world with all sorts of esoteric hints to it in terms of, you know, it's sort of like Romans 1:20, if Travis is up to that. It certainly is a bizarre question, and Harry is flummoxed. He doesn't get this question. He wants a password so he can just walk through. And Luna explains you have to answer the question or wait for someone to help, and Harry says we can't wait, and Luna says,

"No, I see what you mean," said Luna seriously, "well then I think the answer is that a circle has no beginning."

"Well reasoned," said the voice, and the door swung open.

It's going to take us half an hour to unpack that answer, but what I love is that Luna is kind of off-hand with this esoteric wisdom which is penetrating, profound, insightful, and yet a throwaway, almost a comic throwaway. That's what I love about Luna. That's my favorite scene that she's in.

James: I like that too, John. "And that's how you learn," you know. Never mind that every second is precious and it's a matter of life or death. "That's how you learn."

My favorite is near the end of *Order of the Phoenix* when Harry has, that very night, tried to contact Sirius through the mirror, to no avail, has talked to Nick, to no avail, and then he rounds a corner and comes across Luna quite unexpectedly. And Luna is posting the request for her stolen items to be returned, and has that wonderful conversation with Harry, which has a lot more to do with items that have been lost that will be returned to us in the end. I mean people whom we lose, our very lives eventually that we'll lose.

Everything will turn up in the end, and then she is amazed that Harry can't believe he'll, or at least he's not sure if he'll see his lost loved ones again. Of course I'll see my Mom again, she says, and it's just a wonderful conversation, and he feels that sorrow and pain for her and it gets him beyond his own grief; it gets him outside himself. And like with Dobby, with the loss of Dobby, that grief that he feels blocks the Dark Lord's thoughts for him and changes him forever, the basic decision of Book 7, the Horcruxes over Hallows.

And this too is a transcendent moment, and they have that wonderful conversation , and then everything will turn up in the end, and yet I wanted to pack tonight, she says, but Harry wanted to see Sirius again that night, but , you know, there will be a time, and meanwhile, let's just go and have some pudding, and that's just what they do.

Travis: Yeah, and that scene that you mentioned [at Dobby's funeral] is actually my favorite Luna scene because obviously it's just the most painful, to me the most painful scene in the series. Luna is the one that comes in just calmly and she's the one that shuts his eyes and she's the one who says we ought to say something at the grave and ends up being I think almost the only one who says anything and she says

"Thank you so much, Dobby, for rescuing me from that cellar, it's so unfair that you had to die when you were so good and brave. I'll always remember what you did for us. I hope you're happy now."

And there's that calm faith that Luna has that in the face of even the tragedy of death that she's just, you know, we'll see you again, it'll turn up.

James: Now he could be sleeping.

Travis: Right, now he could be sleeping, what a great line.

James: It is, yeah, it is.

John: "I can't believe that you don't believe you'll see her again" is about his mother. She's already at the spot that Harry has to get to.

James: Yeah. Absolutely.

Travis: Yeah.

John: But, guys, this is pretty dense indeed for Luna Lovegood. (laughter)

James: We are talking about Luna.

John: That's right. This is the lady wearing a lion's head...

James: That's right.

John: I mean in every scene with Luna there's a lot of comedy. This is the Luna that calls the Quidditch match and goes on about Losers Lurch and who goes on about the Rotfang Conspiracy... This is one of the great funny characters in fantasy literature. And that's certainly one of the reasons that they love her – more than the esoteric and the transitional and the noumenal Luna. There's just the Luna that, like Ron says, you know, "who always gives good value." She's there for the laugh and for the turn-your-thinking-upside-down-moment or appearance in the books.

James: That's really what I like, the way Rowling turns <u>us</u> upside-down with Luna. I mean we see her reading upside-down, but she's not. She's reading right side up, or what she's reading, you know. She has to turn the book upside down to read it the right way. One of my favorite quotes from *Walden*, in *Walden*, when Thoreau says some people can't tell the difference between a half wit and a wit and a half. Some people can't tell the difference between someone who reads upside down and who reads the right way. You know, we have to learn to read her, and I think we all pick up on it fairly quickly. And she's a delight to read.

John: That's a good point. Because I think most people, when they think about Luna, their first impression is Hermione's view– the kind of skeptical "you-can-do-better-than-that-Harry" type of thing. And yet when we think a little bit more, when we review the books and see where she comes up, I mean we hear about her first in *Goblet of Fire* when they're about to head off to the first World Cup and we meet her in *Half Blood Prince*. But when she appears in *Deathly Hallows*, she actually pulls Harry's fat out of the fire there where he can't conjure a Patronus, and she appears mysteriously to pull him through that, and at the battle at the Ministry in *Phoenix*, she's heroic. She's there with the best of Dumbledore's Army. There's great, great depth to her in addition to the comedy and fun.

James: John, you mention the mention of the Lovegoods in *Goblet of Fire* at the World Cup. They had already arrived, they were already there. That is the first reference to the Lovegood name in the series, I take it.

John: I think so.

James: I've always wondered what their tent would look like, by the way. Which reminds me, as one of my students said two or three years ago, isn't it hard to believe that Harry and Ron don't know about Luna since she's in Ginny's year and she's been around Hogwarts for three years at this point, when they finally say, who's this girl, you know, uh, is that a little hard to believe, does that make you suspect she came to Rowling late, she came to Rowling's mind late?

John: She's a mythic character. And this personality, because it's hard to get a mythic character and be believable and admirable, someone you'd relate to until you have enough engagement with the story. Otherwise it would be like a ghost appearing in a detective novel. You'd be like, this doesn't belong here. Until you the reader are thoroughly engaged, this oth-er-worldly, sort of noetic intelligence appearing on the scene is going to appear a little too loopy, a little too loony.

She appears instead in the flesh in the darkest night of the book, in *Order of the Phoenix*, and it's such a gritty, gritty book, with Umbridge and Harry's disso-lution and breakdown that Luna there appears a little bit like the moon in the sky in the middle of the dark-ness. I mean she sees the light there. She appears at just the right moment where she's believable because the novel is so gritty and realistic and naturalistic, it's straight out of Northrup Frey, it's the allegorical ex-perience . This is the stuff you recognize, the pain you recognize from high school, or whatever, and in that spot, the mythic character works the way it wouldn't have worked in *Goblet*, or *Prisoner*, or ...

Travis: Your mentioning of a ghost in a detective story I think is interesting because if you think about when the member of the Baskerville family showed up to Sherlock Holmes and said, look I think this oth-er detective is actually better than you, and Sherlock Holmes gets all offended, but I came to you because you're someone who's not ..uh..you're not going to rule out a supernatural explanation for something. Isn't that what Luna is, I mean, Luna is the outside explana-tion . She's the one who believes a bunch of weird stuff, she's the fairytale character for the wizarding world itself. Which is already magical.

John: You're the Fay expert here, Travis. Can you put Luna in the context of English fantasy literature?

Travis: I think it's important to do so. My thesis on Luna is that Luna is to the wizarding world what the wizarding world is to us, in a sense. You've got to kind of back up a little bit and think what the fairy tale is and I always go to great thinkers like Chesterton and Tolkien and Madeleine l'Engle who talked about the

fairy tale, who all believed that fairy tales are absolutely necessary for adults . They're not just for kids.
And Chesterton would argue that they're more necessary for the grownup than they are for the kid, I mean
he talks about how a three year old is told that a door
is opened and it's full of wonder and excitement – oh
the door is open, someone opened a door -- but the
twelve year old has to be told that the door was opened
and that there was a dragon, to have any kind of excitement, because we lose our sense of wonder very
quickly about the world.

Tolkien would say that one of the great gifts of the
fairy story is recovered sight. You go into this magical
world, and you 're able to explore the stuff that's going on in our own world in this magical setting and
come back remember now, as Chesterton said, that the
world is a startling place, rather than this sort of mundane thing that we go through in our daily existence.

Well, the question then comes up, what does a magical world do for that, are they all just full of wonder?
Well no, it's got its own version of mundane, it's got its
own version of its daily business and it's not all that excited about the world around it, and thinking "It's full
of wonder," so what do you do? Well, you've got a character like Arthur Weasley who, for him, the Muggle
world is the fantasy world. He's playing around with
spark plugs and cars and all sorts of stuff, and so you
have that sort of thing.

There's this great story by Neil Gaiman where there's
this guy set in his fantasy world and he's struggling
with what he's going to write, and he wonders if he's
going to write some sort of realism and he finally decides to write about fantasy and it turns out fantasy is
about brief case and business suits and business meetings, and so you could go that way, but it doesn't work
that way in the Wizarding world because there's this
political issue where the wizarding world is in hiding
because they were oppressed by Muggles and so most

of the Wizarding world apart from the weird people like Arthur Weasley aren't going to look at the Muggle world and say "yeah, that's a fantastic world, that's full of amazing things that we're not used to in our daily life," so what do you do?

Well, Rowling came along with *The Tales of Beadle the Bard* and in my opinion the only story in that – and they're all great – the only story in that collection that's somewhat boring is 'Babbity Rabbity,' and the reason that it is compared to the other stories, and I love all of them, is as Dumbledore says in his commentary, it's the only one that follows the laws of the already existing magical world. So the other four stories, which I think are fantastic, all have magic, but it's a different kind of magic than the Wizarding world would normally encounter, so they still need that sort of different world to step into which is the gift of the fairy tale that Tolkien says is so important.

Luna is *that* on a daily basis for everyone that knows her. I mean she believes weird stuff. She believes crazy stuff. Nargles and that sort of thing, and she seems crazy to most people, but you can pick on her belief in stuff you can't see all you want, but she's the one, as we said, who can stick her head into the scene where stuff has happened, and she can bring peace and calm into that situation. She's the one who has faith that it's all going to be well in the end. And so you can pick on her faith in the unseen, but Luna isn't easily dismissed. You're going to have to wrestle with Luna, with the type of a character like Luna who is for the Wizarding world what fairytales are for us – sort of a recovery of faith, a recovery of spiritual vision, or the ability to see that the world is a lot more exciting than we tend to think it is on a daily basis.

John: Just following that, Travis, which is wonderful: Is this why Luna's Patronus is a rabbit? (laughter)

Travis: Yes, that's exactly why, in fact I was just revisiting this earlier. Why is her Patronus a hare? Well,

I think Rowling gave us a tip in a 2005 interview when she made the comment that Luna is the kind of person that can believe 10 impossible things before breakfast, which is a reference to the White Queen's telling Alice, in *Alice in Wonderland,* that you should practice, I used to practice 6 impossible things before breakfast every single day. It's not long after that, of course that she has her first interaction with the Mad Hatter and the March Hare where they seem absolutely crazy to her, but in fact may be the only sane ones.

James: Luna's feelings toward Harry. Think back to the mistletoe. And Harry jumps out of the way. And it's a good thing, because there might be nargles there. And think back to how she reacts when he asks her to go to Slughorn's party and then the reports from others about how thrilled she was , how excited she was, and so forth. ... Luna's a girl, she's human, she's not totally lunar. You guys ever had any thoughts about her possibly fantasizing a little about Harry? Did she really want to be kissed?

Travis: You can probably find a lot of that in fan fiction.

James: Yeah, yeah, I've never looked... (laughter)

John: No, I would disagree about her not being totally lunar. And the reasons I disagree are on two counts: One is the scene in the ziggurat, when Harry goes to her bedroom to find out what's going on, really, he finds she's not there, and then sees the ceiling, where the friends are all linked with these golden chains or whatever. Certainly she's human, and she's excited about Harry and this and that, but that scene where all of her friends are joined with these golden links -- sort of friendship illuminated, gold being solid light, point to the importance of her name, Luna, meaning 'moon.'

Again, Luna is really a mythic character. And it's not so much that she's goofy; it's that she belongs to an entirely different sphere of reality. For that to make sense you've got to get to Rowling's medievalism here, I mean, essentially the whole magical world is a pointer to these sixteenth and seventeenth century radical reformation characters, the Seekers, the Muggletonians, and Cambridge Platonists. Those real-world people of the English Renaissance, like the magical world, still see the world as basically three spheres.

You have the terrestrial world, which is fallen, the earth, which is subject to change and degeneration. Next you have the Lunar sphere, which is transitional, a holding point between the fallen and the perfect. Last you have you have the reality beyond the moon which is ether and perfection and the music of the spheres, etc.

That Lunar sphere, that boundary between the ethereal and the fallen terrestrial world we live in, is the perspective that Luna brings to the story. She's this other-worldly character that always seems to be goofy to them , but she's almost like an icon, the thing through which you see, and through which these other-worldly referents shine through. Just like the moon in the darkness again. Luna consequently doesn't really bond with the characters. She doesn't dance with anybody...

James:...Right – she dances alone...

John:...that's right. When she comes to the wedding, first of all she has to arrive as Luna, the moon, but she arrives in solar colors "bright yellow robes... with a sunflower in her hair." As gold and light, the moon reflecting the sun, Luna arrives at the alchemical wedding as the resolution of contraries. She's both solar and lunar, and she dances alone and beautifully, "giving good value."

(laughter) And this appearance, in the beginning of that book, that's the pointer to where Harry has to arrive at in the end. He has to reach that kind of resolution of contraries. In a way she's the foil to Hermione, whose thinking we can talk about later, but, back to

James' point, no, I don't think she wants to be Harry's girlfriend. Forgive me, this may really upset fandom, but I really was almost disappointed when Rowling assigned her a mate. I thought she's so far beyond any of the other characters...

James: Newt's grandson, right?

John: Travis, what do you think of that? She's got an alchemical meaning as well, but I think the first meaning Luna's name obviously has, her name meaning 'the moon,' her first name has to be astrological. The first thing there, and that gets you that first lunar/ sublunar distinction that she represents, as you said earlier about Fay, a sense of wonder to the magical world. She's a light shining in the darkness.

Travis: Yes absolutely, and I think to support that even more, and to kick it back to you actually, and the connection that you made with Elizabeth Gouge's story in *Harry Potter's Bookshelf* -- we should be talking about that.

John: Right. Rowling points to Goudges' *Little White Horse* and says that was her favorite story as a child, and, more important, that it was almost a template for the *Potter* books. It's a little mysterious when you read it how Ms. Rowling used it as a template until you see the astrological and alchemical scaffolding that I explain in *Bookshelf*. There's Sir Benjamin Merriweather that Goudge calls the "solar Merriweather," and then there's Loveday Mannette. who is the lunar counterpoint in the novel. Clearly the Lovegood part in Luna's name is the pointer to the Loveday in Loveday Mannette.

But these women have an alchemical meaning in both *White Horse* and *Harry Potter*. Luna appears at the beginning of the alchemical crisis in Harry's life, *Order of the Phoenix*, the nigredo or nadir of the series. James's favorite scene, with Harry and Luna at the end of that book, is the key transition between the black novel and the white novel of the series. Luna, the moon, is a traditional alchemical symbol of the white stage of the alchemical work. Luna, Harry's friend, represents in his story this time of purification alchemists call the *albedo*. This is the alchemical stage in which all the big changes in the hero have to happen for Harry to be prepared for the crisis of the last stage, the *rubedo*, in which all these changes will be revealed. Harry's *albedo* happens in *Half Blood Prince*, which is where Luna makes her biggest appearances. That's where she's in Dumbledore's Army, where she's Harry's date ...that book is Luna's novel the way it is Albus Dumbledore's. It's the white book in the series.

James: Luna never lies. Almost every significant character in the entire series tells a lie, great or small, for good or ill. But Luna never lies, does she?

Travis: I can't think of an instance.

John: You're absolutely right. Dumbledore on down. Everybody lies.

Travis: Even when she's uncomfortable, Luna never lies.

John: Yeah, because she's fearless. Luna's not really of this terrestrial plane. And the thing that everybody else takes as their marker and reference, fear of death, she does not. She almost embraces death. She looks forward to meeting the people on the other side of the veil. She has the confidence about the fabric of reality, that she's a part of it, and that she will continue beyond this sublunary sphere that she happens to have dropped into. Why lie?

Travis: It's that transcendent nature, I mean she's beyond our need ... We're back to Gothic literature, and Gothic literature signifying that there's something wrong with the world, and Luna is transcendent, she knows that there's something wrong with the world, but she is in some ways separate from it. She doesn't feel the need to lie and take part in this stuff that's wrong with the world. She's beyond it.

James: And another aspect of being transcendent as far as the social world of Hogwarts is concerned, is that she's immune to embarrassment. As the Fall term began in some of my classes at Pepperdine, some of the students have a problem with Luna's character – bear in mind these are 18 year old people – because they don't think that's credible. You can't be that immune to peer pressure and embarrassment. And, again, when you're 18, that seemed to be the consensus in the class. I can understand that. I think it's an acquired immunity that it takes a few decades to be – not to be embarrassed when others might be . But Luna is never embarrassed. Others may be embarrassed that she's not embarrassed. Like when Harry hears her say, "it's almost like having friends…" Dumbledore's Army.

John: And also that transcendent quality gives her this ability to deliver one-liners with the deadpan voice that is hilarious. In moments of absolute crisis, she talks as if she's at tea. There's the Malfoy Manor basement, where … "I think we have a nail." Ron is going wall to wall, and screaming, and "Yeah, I think we have the answer here." But my favorite is when she drops Carrow with a curse in the Ravenclaw common room and looks at Harry and says, "Who would have thought it would make so much noise?" She's essentially killed an adult and a teacher and she comments on the *noise* …

Travis: The one-liners, like the Rot Fang conspiracy and such is exactly why Harry ends up being so happy he brought her to Slughorn's party, which was an uncomfortable mess, with the biographer and Sanguini, and all that, and the incident with Malfoy and Snape and in the midst of all this mess where Harry doesn't want to be that close to Slughorn in the first place because he just wants to collect him and all that , here's Luna delivering these one-liners about the Rot Fang conspiracy and he's just cracking up.

John: And what a change that represents. She again is this point of transition and change in the books. Remember when Harry's hanging on Cho's every glance, and Cho comes into the Gryffindor compartment on the Hogwarts Express. There's Neville and Luna and Harry's thinking, "oh gosh, of all the people I'd want to be seen with it's not these two losers." But then by *Half Blood Prince*, Harry chooses her as his date when he's the King of the world. At this point everyone loves him, everyone believes him, he's the Chosen One, and he's chosen her.

And how fitting, because she's this transcendent figure, and Harry has gotten some aspect of what James has been talking about here, this kind of indifference to other people's opinion. Harry recognizes that quality. When any other girl in the school would die for his attention. One tries to drug him to get him to fall in love with her and he chooses Luna who is impervious to those kinds of concerns.

Travis: Whether Harry realizes it at the time, I mean, John, you've done a lot of work on the eye symbolism, and Harry's problem is that he doesn't see rightly. Luna already does. Her eyes are spoken of a lot. She's the first person who can see thestrals that we know of, she's the first person who can see things that we can't see, she has the vision that Harry ends up needing.

John: Right. And we see her with funny glasses, as James has said, she's reading upside-down but really she's seeing things correctly, she sees thestrals, but my favorite is that at the wedding, she sees through Harry's disguise. He's Barney, and she says she recognizes him because of his "expression." But of course his expression isn't Harry's expression. It's Barney's. And that ability to see beyond the surface, or to see things beyond the veil, ties into Rowling's theme throughout these books that's there's an inside that's bigger than the outside.

Travis: It's part of her subversive anti-materialism. There's a spiritual reality to the world.

James: Of all the characters in the series, I'm really surprised at how often I think of her. When I was teaching Emerson's *Self Reliance*, the whole element of non-conformity and integrity, I mean Luna may never have read Emerson's *Self Reliance*, but she lives it. And then just about a week ago we did *Glass Menagerie* and Laura's character in the Glass Menagerie, the gentleman caller tells Laura at one point, you're different from all other people. Other people are 100 x 1000 and you're 1 x 1. Other people are as common as weeds but you're blue roses. And then Laura says blue is wrong for roses, and he says, but it's right for you. Times like that I think of Luna Lovegood. That wonderful, wonderful characterization.

John: That brings us to the contrast with Hermione. By the time we meet Luna we've had Hermione for 4 plus books it seems, and she and McGonagall embody this linear, masculine, deductive intelligence. Enter Luna, who is none of those things. In Greek Hermione is *episteme*, she's science, she's rock hard. And then Luna comes in and she's *sophia*. She's Wisdom. She's this insight, this feminine quality which is non-linear, intuitive, in philosophical language, noetic. In the resolution of those contraries, Harry loves them both. He doesn't say, "Hermione, you're a ditz and Luna really has it right," but he also won't dismiss Luna. And we get that in the Lovegood ziggurat where Hermione shows how masculine and linear and restricted she is in her thinking .

Travis: That's exactly the scene. You've got Hermione versus the Lovegoods where the *Tale of the Three Brothers* is being told. Rowling kind of plays a trick on us to get us on Hermione's side because Hermione's arguing with Xenophilius about the horn whether it's an Erumpent horn or not, and Hermione is right. But then Harry hears the Tale and he's off on another one of his crazy quests, like proving Malfoy was a Death Eater in *Prince*, and Hermione is saying, "this can't be real, it's a fairy tale, it's just a story." She's arguing the hard line that there's no evidence, there's no logic, and we buy into it because of the Horn.

Rowling's played this bait-and-switch trick on us because Hermione has gotten too old in her thinking. She just five years earlier was arguing with Binns on the other side of it, saying, well there's some truth to the legend of the Chamber of Secrets, aren't legends built on truth? Now she's completely dismissing the truth of the Hallows because it's a legend. And so this argument between Hermione-knowledge and Lovegood-wisdom sets up the trip to Malfoy Manor and Harry's crisis with the eye in the mirror there. Harry ends up being the resolution, rising from Dobby's grave, and his decision from that point onwards reflect that Harry finally has gained the knowledge and wisdom he needs to defeat Voldemort.

John: And the irony of that argument with Xenophilius, of course, is that Hermione the empiricist denies the existence of the Hallows of which she's had six years experience...

Travis: She's been hiding under one of them for the past six years!

James: And by the way, give Ron some credit too, because he appreciates both women.

Travis: Rare is the moment when we can appreciate Ron's contribution. Gentlemen, we're out of time! Thank you for a wonderful conversation and good night to you and to the Pundits out there in the audience. Write and tell us what you think at the PotterCast page of Leaky Cauldron!

CHAPTER 2

Christmas at Hogwarts

Thoughts About Nativity and Harry Potter

TRAVIS PRINZI: WE'RE HERE to talk about
Christmas. Christmas has an important place
in the plot of the HP books. Book by book, you never go through a book without a Christmas being the
occasion for something exciting. Usually something
important to the plot of that book, but I think we're
going to see throughout our discussion here, not only
to the plot of each book, but it gives some sort of foreshadowing or set-up for the big payoff at the end with
one of the most intense scenes of the book, which is
the Christmas finale of the whole series in *Deathly
Hallows.*

We'll talk about *Deathly Hallows,* then, but let's
back up first and we'll talk at first about Christmases
as a setting. James, you wanted to talk a bit about
the Christmas setting and the weather involved, and
something as simple as the atmosphere created by
that. Why don't we start from there.

James Thomas: Yeah, I think this really caught
my attention upon re-reading because I've lived in
California for almost 30 years, Southern California,

and you appreciate an author who creates the weather, Christmas-weather, to be almost a character. And weather in Scotland, or in Grimauld Place, wherever, it is cold. Weather is a factor. I think I say somewhere in *Repotting Harry Potter*, that where I live now, weather, if personified in a play, is a bit player with very few if any lines, standing hat in hand at the back of the stage. Weather in Harry's world is like a bad Lear, a raging actor Lear, center stage screaming at you. Whether it's a bad Quidditch day or whatever. So this is so much part of the Christmases – the claustrophobic setting, the cold creeping in through the corners...

Another thing about setting and atmosphere with regard to Christmas is that it marks time; it's a major watershed, breaking point, milestone in the academic year. They look forward to it, look forward to the few days of vacation, look forward to seeing each other, being reunited when they all come back. I like the way it affords us a smaller cast of characters who have remained at Hogwarts during Christmas in those books which they do, which means no classes, no Quidditch, no crowds, no complications and important things can happen involving sometimes just a few people, like the Poly-juice caper, and so forth.

And one more thing comes to mind – the treatment of Christmases overall I think enables us to see an 11-year-old child's Christmases evolve. Here's a child who was denied the thrills of Christmases for almost a decade. Denied a decade of gifts and anticipation and excitement when he was Dursleyed out of his Christmases for all that time. And then Harry begins to get and give gifts, great and small, from mismatched socks to the Firebolt and the annual Weasley sweater, and the reader gets six good Harry Christmases as he gradually gets this part of his childhood back and Christmases revealed and restored to him. He's finally among those – not those who raised him because they had to take him in -- but he's among those whom he loves and who love him. And what reader doesn't almost feel compelled to say out loud, "Merry Christmas, Harry!" He deserves it; he finally experiences Christmas.

Travis: It's interesting that *Harry Potter and the Sorcerer's Stone* gets shown every Christmas on television, because that moment is so potent, I think people feel it. It's not a Christmas movie start to finish, but every Christmas season, that movie gets played because that moment is so potent for viewers and for readers.

James: Isn't that wonderful? You know, every one of us remembers as kids waiting every day of December. We wait 23 or 24 days for the magic, and Harry has waited again almost a decade to experience that entitlement of childhood.

John: "Always winter and never Christmas." The point that James makes about Christmas being a character, and a dark character, even Lear on steroids, that points to the fact that, Harry, while he does have some warmth around Christmas, he does receive gifts and there is some kindness to it, still almost every one of the Christmas seasons is disturbing, as much as anything else.

We get the beginning discomfort, which comes from the isolation and him no longer living with the context of the school in session. But, if we check through all of the Christmases and just roll through the books for those chapters, I think we see there's adventure and there's darkness.

That Mirror of Erised scene, where he gets the Invisibility Cloak and he runs off to see the Mirror of Erised, that's a crusher at first. Yes, he gets to see his family and everything, but he almost gets broken there. It's critical to the whole book what happens in front of that mirror.

In *Chamber* we have the Poly-juice potion and mistaken identity, things aren't really what they seem to be at Hogwarts. Then we have the fight in *Prisoner of*

Azkaban between Ron and Hermione at Christmas …I think Travis' calling this Yule "excitement" is misrepresenting it; we're miserable.

In *Goblet* you have the Yule ball and we have another fight with Ron and Hermione and Hagrid's real identity is revealed. And *Phoenix* is the real mad one. The whole reason of being inside Grimauld Place at Christmas instead of Hogwarts is that Harry has been inside Nagini's head attacking Mr. Weasley. It's a frightening thing – visit St. Mungo's? This is a bizarre thing, with Lockhart, the Longbottoms, and the soon-to-be-dead Bode.

The only truly "family Christmas" that Harry has is at the Weasleys' in *Half Blood Prince* and it's not a happy one, either. We have them fighting about Snape's identity and whether he's the good guy or the bad guy, Fleur hating the music, a visit from Scrimgeour.

I suppose this is what Christmas is supposed to be, in a sense. There's a light shining in the darkness, but as you said, James, the weather and the environment, it's cold, it's isolated, it's kind of scary. There's a light shining, but it's cold and she seems to be emphasizing the darkness. That brings us to the *Deathly Hallows* Christmas nightmare.

Travis: That's it exactly. Rowling doesn't do anything really overtly religious. She's not telling the Nativity story. But she's giving us the feel of that same story. I argue that there's almost a Christmas to Easter pattern, almost a Liturgical calendar pattern happening from book to book. Something exceedingly important that's happening is this darkness at Christmas; there's some light that shines in the darkness, like you're saying, and then it leads to that Easter, that symbolic death and resurrection Harry goes through at the end of each book, and of course to the ultimate rising from the dead in the finale.

John: Are the Pundits throwing it out here as a thesis that the Christmases are sort of set-ups for the

Easters in them? As you said, Travis, Harry dies in every book in the presence of a symbol of Christ and rises from the dead (in three days in *Philosopher's Stone* –she's not being especially difficult about that). Are all of these set-ups for Harry's faux death and resurrection after he goes through the Forbidden Forest and returns from King's Cross?

That's the big victory for Harry in *Deathly Hallows*. Are the Christmases then set-ups, too, for the Christmas in *Deathly Hallows*? Ms. Rowling said in an interview that the Scriptural passages in Godric's Hollow epitomized the meaning of the entire series. Are we getting, in all the other Christmases, pointers to that *Deathly Hallows* scene?

James: Yeah, I think so. Let's start from the first. You've got the twins throwing snowballs at the turban in *Stone*. It's a boyhood activity. It's Christmas, it's fun. And also a very frosty Christmas, I mean frosty, the very use of the word – Frosty the Snowman, Frosty is a happy word, dashing through the snow, and the frosty relationship, the icy, the cruelty of what Percy does to his mother and the rest of the family in *Prince* and that ominous conversation that takes place out there in the snowy garden between Harry and the Ministry. Light and happy traditional Christmas things are going on simultaneously with very, very serious, dark things.

Travis: And great setup there in those conversations about Snape where Harry makes the comment "No one's that good an actor, not even Snape." The other great comment he makes is when he says that "My Dad used *levicorpus* on Snape" and by the end of the book Harry is also using Snape's curses against him. I think John is right, then, that each book does point to the darkness of *Deathly Hallows* and maybe it would be best to do it book by book and explore that. Does that sound good?

The main event of *Sorcerer's Stone* or *Philosopher's Stone* -- the Invisibility Cloak, the Mirror, the whole interaction there, and his family, in what ways do these point to the final book? I suggest for starters that the mirror at least is very symbolic of the Hallows themselves, and Harry has to face the same dilemma with the mirror in *Deathly Hallows*. He has to know about it, know what it does, so that he will not use it for himself. And using that device properly ends up defeating Volemort. So there's the setup there.

John: And that's great, but there's a more obvious one, in that the Mirror of Erised points us to where Harry looks into it and sees his identity in his family, what he wants, desires, and then he sees himself at the end and transcends that in order to do the right thing to get the Philosopher's Stone. And in *Deathly Hallows* we get Sirius' mirror fragment where he sees the eye.

That is his identity, and he denies it at book opening, on Privet Drive and then he denies it *again* at Christmas. He denies Dumbledore and Dumbledore's love for him after his wand is broken. Harry insists that Dumbledore never loved him and that's the nadir, that's the depth of the nigredo in the seventh book. This near despair is really a consequence of that Mirror and Harry's refusing to see who he really is in the eye reflecting back at him.

We know who he *really* is because we've seen what happened to that Memorial in the Godric's Hollow common, transform itself on Christmas Eve into what is essentially a crèche. We see the loving family and the Harry-child, if you will, which without too much of a stretch on Christmas Eve, we see the Christ child and the Holy Family. No one mistakes this, right?

It's Christmas Eve, the snow's falling, this is a Dickens moment. Harry recognizes himself there, but he doesn't get it. He doesn't understand those scriptural passages. Every great hero's journey has the trip to the dead. Odysseus makes it, Aeneas makes it, Dante, of course, makes an epic of it and all of them go to the dead to get answers to their questions.

Hermione and Harry have got questions here, too; they're trying to find Bathilda Bagshot, but they wind up going through the Kissing Gate beside the Church, which Gate is a portal, and they wind up with the dead. The dead give them answers. Harry gets the scriptural passages that Rowling says epitomize the whole series; he doesn't have a clue about what to make of them, but he gets his answers. "Is that something a Death eater has said?" Harry really turns the St. Paul passage on its head.

Travis: And the wording there is great. Because he doesn't respond properly or as he should with the right information and, as it says, the light in the church went out and then they walk out and they go into this whole ...

John: ...and they meet the serpent

Travis: That's right... the serpent waiting to devour the prophesied vanquisher of evil which I think is from Revelation 12 ...

John: That I think is Rowling's point. I mean, this chapter, outside of 'The Silver Doe,' may be her most brilliant piece of writing. This chapter combines the scene in the graveyard and then the one with Nagini doing the *Alien* number with Bathilda Bagshot, which combination – death, grief, rotting corpses, surprise attack, revisiting a double-murder of immediate family – is a powerful depiction of Christmas Eve as the darkest night of the year, the blackness before the Light comes into the world.

This Christian observance of the darkness of the world before Nativity she combines with the alchemical *nigredo* of *Deathly Hallows*. The first stage, the black stage, in which Harry is the stone's matter which is being shaped, Harry has to be broken down into prime matter. He has to be totally dissolved and dissolute. Everything has to be taken from him. All of his sense of identity has to be broken down. And Ms.

Rowling links that with Christmas Eve in a way which is absolutely brilliant.

As you say, the light in the church goes out, Harry is clueless about what all these things on the tombstones mean, Hermione is trying to understand all these things without success, Harry denies that there is any life after death, all of which things he has to learn before the end.

Of course, who takes him into the Forbidden Forest? His parents walk beside him in the Forbidden Forest. There's no doubt that there's life after death when Harry goes to meet his own death. And yet in this graveyard scene, he's terrified of death. He wants to join his parents, he wishes it was all over, and is as low as you can go. Then we have his meeting with the serpent, the breaking of his wand, and his denial of Dumbledore's love. And we are at last at the very bottom.

We're ready to start coming out of it, ready to begin the ascent with the Silver Doe, Ron's return, and the reintegration of the trio. But we have to be totally broken down. Rowling does this poetically at the darkest time of the year, Christmas Eve, when Harry sees the death of his parents in Voldemort's mind.

You think to yourself, "Gosh this is Christmas?" This is not Bing Crosby. No one sung Jingle Bells during Rowling's trip through this. (laughter) But it's so powerful. She captures, she links, as you wrote in *Harry Potter and Imagination* so well that she links Christmas and Easter and you have to be broken down, you have to face the dragon at Christmas so that the stone can be rolled away at Easter.

James: And we were talking about Book 1. (Laughter)

Travis: Now the Book 2 pointer

James: Wait, wait, wait. One more thing about Book 1. We started with the Mirror. But what about the Invisibility Cloak? What does Dumbledore give Harry when he gives him that? His father had worn this, had been under it, that tactile proof that James Potter was, that he existed, and that private moment that Harry seeks. That's beautiful, too.

Travis: Yes, and it's the first time, really, that he can choose to go alone. And he didn't take Ron with him that first night. He chose to go alone.

John: And where does he go?

James: To the library. Heh heh.

John: Oh that's right.

Travis: To the restricted section. That's the first place he goes.

John: On to the next book?

Travis: Yeah. *Chamber of Secrets.* What's the pointer to *Deathly Hallows'* finale there? It seems obvious enough if we're talking about this Poly-juiced Hermione and Harry walking into Godric's Hollow. The pointer in *Chamber* is obvious enough.

John: That's the book in which they first do Poly-juice potion and (at Christmas time) and head to the Common Room of the bad guys. Just like at Godric's Hollow where Hermione expects to be attacked by the Dark Lord. It's a clear foreshadowing of what we're to see in the last book.

Travis: And only two of them go. First it's Harry and Ron. And now it's Harry and Hermione.

James: It's just a little off the subject of Christmas but does Poly-juice ever really work as ideally intended? They don't get the information from Draco. They're seen as Muggles looking at the Potter home. The seven Harrys. Hermione doesn't even transition. And her plan to stay if Pansy didn't decide to go home … I mean these are not good plans with Poly-juice.

Travis: And they don't seem to get that lesson because in *Chamber* they have a tiny supply of it that took months to brew. In *Deathly Hallows* they have flasks full, they've got vats, you get the idea they're tapping out of kegs, you know.

John: By *Goblet,* it's definitely something you could buy at the Rite Aid. (laughter) *Prisoner?*

Travis: What have we got on *Prisoner?*

John: We have Ron and Hermione separated again. They're fighting over the Firebolt. That's really the first agonizing separation since the fight with the troll in *Stone.* This is the first painful look at what life is like when Ron and Hermione split. That's really the context of the *nigredo* in *Deathly Hallows.* Again ... Ron's gone.

Goblet, in contrast, is kind of a freak show among Harry's Christmases. It's almost a happy time, no?

Travis: This is the only one where it's not a quiet Christmas. This is loud. Everybody's there and there's a concert, there's a dance going on. There are three different schools there...

John: We do have a split between Ron and Hermione. We have the famous row where Ron pretty much all but says he's in love with Hermione. Hagrid's thing is kind of the only truly dark moment at Christmas. We get Rita outing Hagrid as a half-giant. That causes some repercussions. But Christmas in the fourth book isn't that dark an event. In terms of *Hallows* parallels, we may have to call this the singing inside the church. This is a happier side.

Travis: Is this the setup for how dark it's going to turn? I mean she's not making it quite as dark at Christmas because this is the first book where Harry doesn't win at the end. At the end of this book, Voldemort wins.

John: Good point. It's a trick. If you're jolly at Christmas, it better be one to remember in the graveyard. Good point. Because it is the turning point, what is often called chiasm. This is where she turns the corner on the whole series. How fitting that the Christmas there is a happy one, pointing us to the disaster at the end of that book in Little Hangleton's graveyard and really the disaster of Christmas in *Deathly Hallows'* graveyard scene.

James: Which is perhaps a little nicely foreshadowed when McGonagall says, "we're all going to let down our hair." She says with her hair still in a tight bun.

Travis: Although when Hagrid gives her a kiss in *Philosopher's Stone,* she blushes.

John: Book 5's Christmas is like everything in *Order of the Phoenix*: depressing, even nightmarish. Christmas is at Grimauld Place, but Mr. Weasley is there in a basket. We're glad that he's recovered sufficiently to leave St. Mungo's, but, look, the guy has got snake bites all over him and Harry has finally realized there's something really, really wrong. That trip inside Nagini's head and his consequent conversation with Sirius inside Grimauld Place, Harry's one messed up puppy at Christmas time.

That's where we see the first snake attack and the clearest pointer to *Deathly Hallows'* Christmas fun with Bathilda. Maybe Ms. Rowling in writing *Phoenix* had got to the point where she's already laid out her pointers to *Deathly Hallows.* But that scene in *Phoenix* that takes us out of Hogwarts, back to Grimauld Place in the middle of the night with the Weasleys is the scariest thing that happens to Harry maybe in the whole book. When he doesn't know who he is, and he thinks he may be what's killing people. That's got to be terrible.

Travis: He is very isolated over that Christmas as well because no one will talk to him, and finally Ginny talks him out of it, but he's very isolated.

James: Also what's one of the worst places to be on Christmas Day? The hospital. You've got Mr. Weasley getting better. And you've got the comic relief of those people domestic dispute kind of things, people with hands coming out of their chests. But you've got Gilderoy and it's still a bit of comic relief.

But then Neville's parents. And that's "the most un-funny thing" Harry has ever seen.

John: And Sturgis. We have this set-up with Sturgis. He's about to be killed by his plant

James: Bode is about to be killed

John: Whoops, you're right. But his plant is delivered right there. As you said, there are comic moments there with Gilderoy talking about his loopy handwriting, but between the bubble gum wrappers and the plants about to eat Bode, this is not your Yule log moment with chestnuts roasting..

Travis: *Half Blood Prince* – we're at the Burrow again.

John: I found that a really disappointing trip. It's supposed to be the happiest time. He's with family. He's with friends. Everything's friendly, and yet I found that one of the most depressing Christmas scenes of the whole series. I mean *Deathly Hallows* is mythic in its graveyard and Nagini collage, but this was depressing. Just the radio thing with Mrs. Weasley and the songs she's listening to, annoying the fiancé...

Travis: Mr. Weasley falls asleep.

James: (imitating Fleur) "She's 'orrible."

John: What did you guys think about that scene? Was it really just comic? It seemed like it was just a depressing family thing...

Travis: It is what *Half-Blood Prince is*. It's a back and forth of these comic moments with these really dark moments. And to me the most difficult thing about that entire scene, "Christmas at the Burrow," is when Percy shows up but doesn't really want to be there. You get this hope from Mrs. Weasley, "Oh, he's come back," and then you find out it's all just a game that Scrimgeour is playing and that's hard to take. You know that Percy is a pratt, you know he's got these issues, and you hope he's really going to come back, and you don't get it until the end, it turns out to be a great reunion at the end, but, boy, what a painful thing for them to go through.

John: And as James said we've got that scene with the minister outside where Harry finally really makes it clear he's not the minister's lapdog. Harry the post-adolescent; he 's standing up here as "a Dumbledore man," saying "No way, Rufus." I think Dumbledore actually weeps when he hears about this scene and Harry's loyalty later. This is Harry finally saying "This is where I stand." And it's a great moment.

But at Christmas? I don't know about you, but I don't intend to stand down the equivalent of the President of the United States at my Christmas party. Joyous Noel, it ain't.

Travis: You try to avoid political discussions at Christmas if you can. Who wants to get into those at Christmas? And here's Harry saying "You people never get it right, do you? No matter what side of this thing you're on, you never get it right."

James: And Percy. What a low point for Percy. What a feather in his cap to bring Harry around as the mascot for the Ministry and, oh yeah, see the folks, and drop by his house which of course he doesn't go home to, and we just appreciate even more Percy's return in *Hallows* because of that awful scene for Percy in *Prince*. What is it, *six* people claim to have thrown vegetables at him?

Travis: Did we hit the pointer in *Half Blood Prince* to the last book? What's the pointer here?

John: The whole context of Harry's being at Godric's Hollow is that he has gone rogue from the time he has stood down the Minister of Magic and said I'm not with you but agin' you.

James: "Dumbledore's man through and through."

John: That's right. He's basically declared the context of all that goes on in *Deathly Hallows*.

Travis: Which makes the *Deathly Hallows* Christmas that much more dramatic because at the end of the *Deathly Hallows* Christmas he's saying, "Never mind, I'm not Dumbledore's man."

John: That is, of all the lows that Harry gets in the books, his wand is broken, his phoenix core is shattered, it's not totally broken, he's kept the fragments in his little Mokeskin bag, but his renunciation of Dumbledore, "He never loved me," it's so profound, he's turning his back on this white bearded man in the clouds. It's as low as you can go. Again. To link that message with Christmas and the darkness before the light comes into the world I think is one of Rowling's *Hallows* signatures – alchemical stage with Christian holiday -- and a brilliant one.

Travis: All right, well, there you have the Potter Pundits' take on Christmas in the Harry Potter series. The Christmases from each of the books set up the big Christmas, the intense scene with Bathilda Bagshot and the graveyard and Nagini and all of that happening, Harry's lowest moment in *Deathly Hallows*.

We welcome your comments, corrections and questions at Pottercast.com. We can't wait to have a discussion with you about this. So we hope you'll come on over to Pottercast.com and discuss this with us. And for more information on the Potter Pundits, visit us at potterpundits.com.

CHAPTER 3

Gothic Schoolboy, Part 1

with Dr. Amy H. Sturgis

How Harry Potter Differs from Tom Brown and Billy Bunting and What He Has in Common with Frankenstein and Dracula

TRAVIS PRINZI: BECAUSE IT'S October, and because it's Halloween time, we thought it would be appropriate to give you a couple of segments on scary elements of Harry Potter, particularly Harry Potter, set in the context of Gothic literature, which J.K. Rowling knows well and clearly has worked into her series.

We have a special guest with us this time. We've got our regular pundits and also Amy H. Sturgis, who is an expert on Gothic fiction, and has been teaching Harry Potter courses longer than anybody in academia. We hope you enjoy this show as much as we did making it!

Because this conversation was an hour long, we split it into two segments. Here, then, is the first of our two segments on Harry Potter and Gothic literature. [Scary organ music]

Travis: Welcome to another segment of Potter Pundits! We have a special guest with us tonight along with the regular pundits. We have, of course, author of *The Deathly Hallows Lectures*, John Granger, hello John.

John Granger: Wonderful to be here, Travis.

Travis: And the author of *Repotting Harry Potter*, James Thomas. Hello James.

James Thomas: Hi, Travis.

Travis: And also with us, our special guest pundit this week is fantasy and science fiction scholar Amy Sturgis, who has been teaching Harry Potter classes probably longer than anybody else, since 2003 at Belmont University. So, hello, Amy.

Amy Sturgis: Hi, Travis, thank you for having me with you today.

Travis: Thank you for being with us. We've all got funny Potter name connections here, no? We've got John *Hermione Granger*, right, and then we've got *James Potter* Thomas, and we've got Amy *Sturgis Podmore*, and we've got Travis the *Half-Blood Prinzi*. (groans) Moving right along...

Travis: We're bringing our audience some special programming this time – we hope this will be aired on Pottercast around Halloween time, so it's time to talk about some scary stuff and that sort of thing.

When it comes to Gothic literature, not a ton has been done yet on the Gothic elements in Harry Potter, believe it or not, in fact I think it was in 2008, Jean Cummins' essay, "The Gothic in Children's Literature," was really the first treatment.

At the end of the same year, I published *Harry Potter and Imagination* and in it I did an entire chapter on elements of fear in the fairy tale, and then just a couple months ago, John Granger's *Harry Potter's Bookshelf* was published and he did a Gothic chapter in there. So not a ton of work has been done, but we have a start, and now we have Amy Sturgis with us because she is working on a book called *The Gothic Imaginations of J.R.R Tolkien, Madeline L'Engle and J.K. Rowling* which I am certain is going to be a very fascinating read on the topic of the Gothic with those authors and Harry Potter fans are going to love it. (I should say now so you don't forget it, if you want to keep in touch with Amy and find out when this book is coming out, amyhsturgis.com is where you should go.)

So, Amy, you being the expert on Gothic literature, writing a book on it, can you sort of give us an introduction? I've thrown out the word Gothic several times now and many people may not know what we're talking about, so can you kind of give us a foundation, give us a background, talk to us about what Gothic literature is all about?

Amy: Absolutely. When we think about 'Gothic,' we can go all the way back to the Goths, or we can go back to Gothic architecture, but when we're speaking specifically about Gothic literature, our starting point is 1764 with Horace Walpole's *The Castle of Otranto*. *Castle* had a number of ingredients that Harry Potter fans would recognize, for instance, the old castle and family secrets, and strange things coming out of the woodwork to surprise the heroine and the hero. But Horace Walpole's *Castle of Otranto* is considered to be the first modern work of Gothic literature.

Shortly after *Castle*, Ann Radcliffe became, for all practical purposes, the mother of Gothic literature. She wrote a number of books such as *The Mysteries of Udolpho* (1794), *The Italian* (1797), and quite a few others. She was a best-selling author in her day and in fact, Jane Austen in her *Northanger Abbey*, which is a sort of parody of Gothic literature, brings Radcliffe up in particular as this figure that embodied the Gothic.

There are a lot of other key texts that came out in the late 18th and early 19th centuries that are considered to be the works that set the mold for the Gothic. Books like Matthew Louis's *The Monk* (1796),

William Thomas Beckford's *Vathek* (1786), of course
Mary Wollstonecraft Shelley's *Frankenstein* (1818) and
Charles Maturin's *Melmoth the Wanderer* (1820).

So what do all these books have in common? First,
I want to note that what is Gothic isn't set in stone.
Radcliffe and friends started this first movement to
what we call the Gothic and it has changed over time.
You see how the Romantics, people like Byron and
Coleridge, put their own spin on it. You get things
like vampires coming out of their innovations. We
have the Victorian movements both in Europe, with
people like the Bronte sisters, and in the U.S., people
like Edgar Allen Poe. and eventually through the 20th
century, you get writers like H.P. Lovecraft, and those
who wrote for *Weird Tales*, bringing the Gothic to a
different century with a different modern sensibility.
And of course we have the Gothic all the way up until
today.

But all of these works *do* share certain traits. If I had
to define what the Gothic is, I'd steal a bit from scholar
Jerrold Hogle[1] and say that we can think of four major
ingredients for the Gothic.

- The first ingredient for the Gothic imagination
  would be that it's **rooted in its setting**. An an-
  tiquated space, a claustrophobic place, whether
  it's a castle or even a spaceship. You can think of
  the movie, *Alien*, as a modern re-working of the
  classic Gothic story.

- Also, the Gothic story is **absorbed with the
  past**, either in general…"wow this stuff is old"…
  or with a recent personal past and all the stories
  that make a character who he or she is.

- A third characteristic is the association of
  the story with **secrets that are either literally
  haunting the characters or psychologically
  haunting the characters**. They're either in their
  mind worrying about how these secrets will be

uncovered and what they will mean once the mysteries are solved, or they're really the subject of ghosts and spirits.

- Last of Hogle's four points, the Gothic story is involved with **blurring the line between the natural and the supernatural**, which ends up making the Gothic story a natural parent of the modern science fiction, fantasy, and horror genres.

But there are two more points I'd like to make that we need to keep in mind when we think about how the Gothic tradition relates to Harry Potter.

- **One is something that scholars David Punter and Glennis Byron said,[2] that ever since 1764, when the genre really kicked off, the Gothic has flourished at times of potential or actual social upheaval. In other words, this has been a genre where you have protest, challenging of the status quo, it's giving voice to the voiceless and subversive in one way or another.**

When you think about how this is played out over time, early works written, for instance, by Protestants during the tumultuous time of the Inquisition, dealt in particular with Catholicism. Later works by women novelists are critical of the suffocating restrictions placed on women in male dominated societies. Other Gothic stories penned during the Industrial Revolution reflect fear of dehumanization and urbanization and mechanization. Ms. Rowling is playing into this to give voice to her concerns.

- And lastly, the mother of the Gothic, Ann Radcliffe, said something really interesting about what the Gothic really is in her essay "On the Supernatural in Poetry." She said that we shouldn't think it's just horror, being scared, **it's about terror.** And she said "terror and horror

---

are so far opposite that the first expands the soul and awakens the faculties to a high degree of life. The other contracts, freezes and nearly annihilates them."

In other words, where horror paralyzes the individual, the experience of terror sublimely wakes up the soul to its own power. And I think that's really the story of Harry Potter. About a soul awakening to its own understanding and its own power as Harry grows up and discovers who and what he is, and what choices he must make.

Travis: That's a fantastic introduction, especially as it relates to....

John: "Cut!"

Travis: Yeah, "Cut! We're done!" In one take, too, Amy; you've said it all right there with respect to Harry Potter and the soul. John and I agree, obviously, that Rowling's Potter novels are largely about souls. I've argued that Harry Potter is more than anything else a story about two souls. Some of the Gothic elements that come into that I think are extremely important. So many questions, so many ways we can go there.

John: We should start with the beginning of the books. The way Amy has talked about this, our first experience of the Gothic is the terror that the Dursleys feel when all of a sudden these "messages from no one" begin to appear. We get all these scenes from Hitchcock's *The Birds* when these letters keep coming and coming. And from this mysterious character, "No one;" remember *Stone's* Chapter 3 title, "Letters from No One." We don't know what it's about or where the letters are from, and Harry is mystified and curious. The Dursleys are terrified but Harry's already been living this classic Gothic tale. He's living *Jane Eyre's* nightmare. He's been beaten up by his cousin, he's abused by his aunt...

Amy: ...exactly. Locked up in a little room under the stairs – talk about claustrophobia.

John: That's right. He's in the equivalent of *Jane Eyre's* "red room." Harry basically *is* Jane Eyre to start off, and he goes off to meet Severus Snape, *Harry Potter's* Miss Scratcherd, where he gets the full Jane Eyre experience. But, first, we meet the Gothic when, all of a sudden, the letters from no one come out of nowhere. And it's terrifying.

James: I love that parallel, too, with regard to Normal and Magical which is the natural/supernatural tension in the Gothic. And there's that last bastion of defense against anything that is not Dursley normal and that's the tension with which we begin.

John: That tension really is the premise of the book. *Harry Potter* is a schoolboy novel. That is its core genre. It is not a Gothic novel, per se. But what makes it different from *Tom Brown's School Days* and Enid Blyton's school fiction, the pedestrian schoolboy novel, is that it's saturated with these Gothic elements that Amy is talking about. We get this suffusion of the supernatural so that it's normal. You've got a poltergeist here, you've got a ghost over here, you've got Count Sanguini at the party, you've got a troll in the basement. This is not your normal boarding school (we hope). This is not what Eton is supposed to be about.

Amy: Exactly. And almost immediately we're introduced to these mysteries, these secrets that have been kept from Harry. He discovers not only what he is (he's going to be a wizard), but, wait – his parents didn't die as he was told they died? There's something caught up with this massive war that had taken place that somehow they're involved with. And it's not just the Wizarding world is magical, but his own blood line, his family past, who he is, and what makes him 'who he is' is immediately brought into question, and, really, you spend the next 7 books unraveling all of those secrets.

John: Right. In that origin story for Harry we get the 'tainted blood' and "bond of blood" cliché from the

Gothic, we get the 'confused origin story,' and we get the scar as 'the telltale mark.' I explain in *Bookshelf's* chapter on the Gothic that the Potter story has twenty-five Gothic tokens in its story-line.

The story begins with this avalanche of Gothic markers just to make sure that we readers 'get' it. You've got a boy here with a scar and we don't know where he comes from and it's about his blood. This is as if you have Frankenstein and Dracula walk through the Dursleys' living room. Cue the Gothic story.

James: I have a question for you three. What moment in the series do you first experience real terror? When has Rowling actually moved us to that level, achieved that effect that Poe valued so highly?

John: When asked "are the books getting darker?" after *Order of the Phoenix* was published (because we're basically in the dark that entire book, Rowling herself said the books started off with a double murder and "hey, Voldemort's head on the back of Quirrell's turban is about as terrifying as I can get." Certainly me, when I first read about Voldemort's head on the back of Quirrell's head, I thought "wow."

Travis: And I think she starts just a little bit earlier in that same novel. I wasn't necessarily afraid, I think you're right, I think that's the key intense moment, but the moment when Harry's standing in the forest, and suddenly a cloaked figure stands there with silver blood dripping down its cloak.

Amy: Yes

Travis: ...that's really our first ...

John: ... that would do it...

Amy: And it's terrifying because it's unknown. He can't really see who's there, he just knows there's a shadowy figure, he can't identify a person. Harry can't really see what's happening, and this notion that there's something just beyond the mist there. That's the key to a lot of the mysteries that are all happening. That he can't quite see the unknown aspect of that is I think more frightening than actually seeing ...whoop...the turban's off and now you actually see Voldemort.

John: That Harry freezes, and it makes you think, well maybe it's not that scary, but Draco cues us into what our proper response is supposed to be here. We're supposed to run screaming into the forest "aaaaaah!"

Travis: It is. There's "ahhhhhhh" all across the page

John: Was that your first scene, James?

James: I would have said Quirrell at the end, and certainly when that friendly kid from 50 years ago, Tom Riddle, "Oh, hand me my wand, will you." And he's twirling it there, and then of course the rearrangement of the letters of the name. That's a pretty terrifying moment, too, in *Chamber of Secrets*.

John: And again, in that Quirreldemort scene in *Stone*, in the scene with the Mirror of Erised, we're in the underground, we're in the subterranean passage, we're in a narrow space with this horrific evil, so we get this feeling of terror – not necessarily horror, this is not chain saw massacre stuff. This is the stuff not necessarily that freezes you and strips you of all your understanding. This is terror, which heightens all of your senses, makes you more aware of who you are and what you're about. It actually makes you more sensitive to the way you think about death which to me is the hallmark and point of Gothic: to rub the immediacy of death in your face because we live in a world which denies death.

Really, Amy, Gothic literature grows out of the reaction, as you were saying, to the Industrial Revolution and the simultaneous putting off of the idea of the world as a fallen place and acceptance of the myth of progress: that we're going to somehow have a heaven on earth created by our material circumstances. The Gothic brings death back into the forefront: "Hey, right underneath the carpet there's something ugly and supernatural that wants to kill you, that wants to eat you for breakfast."

Amy: Exactly. And the dead are as much active characters as the living are. Thinning that veil and making that dialogue between the living and the dead makes you think about death all the more.

Travis: Rowling basically brings zombies into her story with her Inferi...

Amy: ...so awesome

Travis: ...so awesome. If you want to talk about the height of terror, the first peak for me is the scene with Voldemort dripping blood down his cloak. But if you want to talk about the height of fear in the story, probably that scene in the cave, when there's suddenly an army of zombies. I mean the idea of the dead coming back is as old as literature. In *Gilgamesh*, Ishtar reminds everybody that there are more dead than the living and says "I'm going to break open the gates of hell, and let the dead out and the dead will outnumber the living." It's a horrifying concept and I think the cave of Inferi scene is very well done.

John: The Inferi don't scare me so much, per se. It's when they take him into the water and I think as a reader "Oh...no... It's scary enough to be carried around by the dead guys, but they're taking me *into the water* -- inside **a cave**." Things are not looking very good there for Harry. You're right, that may be terrific (as that word is meant) climax of the series. Even when Harry is going toe to toe with Voldemort in the Great Hall, I'm thinking, "You know, this isn't so bad compared to the dead guys taking him into the water."

Travis: I think the only competing scene is the snake coming out of Bathilda Bagshot's body. There is a great Gothic high.

Amy: This all makes me think also of one of the other scenes that really hit it for me in terms of making me think of the immediacy of death, and that's, well, first of all, the setting of Grimmauld Place. More important, though, is the experience that Molly Weasley has there with the Bogart in *Phoenix*, where she sees all of her family members dead here in this setting where you have literally people who are dead calling insults at you from their portraits – right? – so the dead are heckling you while you're …

John: Dead house elves, Sirius' mum…

Amy: Exactly. So you've got it coming to you from all sides; the images of your worst fears while the other dead people are heckling you about your fears.

James: I feel that scene much more emotionally during subsequent readings for some reason – to imagine Molly there looking at one after the other of the children, and ironically she's comforted most by Sirius and Lupin who, of course, will not make it through, and they're telling her "We'll make it…" It's a very emotional scene, very powerful, and she's so apologetic, "Sorry, just being silly," where she's just being a loving mother. It's a beautiful scene.

Travis: But I think, on my own reading at least, the first time I ever really considered a boggart potentially frightening, it just seemed comic…

James: Yup. Yeah.

Travis: … but when Molly can't stand one down and is seeing what she's seeing, now the boggart becomes a powerfully scary creature.

James: And another person can't quite appreciate what is terrifying to someone else. Remember one of the girls wonders why Lupin is scared of crystal balls.

John: And in that Hogwarts classroom scene, we see all the students' fears, and they're kind of clichéd phobias. We see big spiders, mummies…but, as a parent, when I see Molly driven to her knees by her dead family, an entirely different experience, when I think to myself, this is probably what I as a daddy would see if the boggart comes out of the desk.

Rowling seems to be doing these Gothic touches not as throw-away moments as she's doing the schoolboy novel. She actually includes full Gothic stories *inside* the schoolboy formula. The stunner to me of the

Gothic story inside the story is when she has, in the middle of the battle of Hogwarts, Harry is trying to find this diadem horcrux and she decides to have, you know, the Ravenclaw ghost decide to tell this Gothic romance about the Bloody Baron. I imagine Harry kind of sitting down, crossing his legs, putting his chin in his hand and listen to this Gothic horror story, which is straight from Ann Radcliffe.

Amy: Exactly.

James: Amy, what do you think the mock Gothic elements might mean? The ones she's clearly inverting or having fun with. Maybe Nearly Headless Nick type things. Is this element strong in the series?

Amy: Yes, I would distinguish, though, the way she does it from the way that, say, Jane Austen did, with *Northanger Abbey*. Because Jane Austen really thought this literature in a way was horrible and she called certain novels "horrible novels" that she mentions in *Abbey*, and plays off of them and was attempting to make a critique by twisting it and tweaking it in that way. And I think Rowling is much more playful than that, lovingly playful.

Nearly Headless Nick is the perfect example, I think, because you have his whole story, and you have his Deathday party and all of these things brought in. Peeves is another one. Also the way she's playful with a lot of notions of what monsters are, when they're actually *not* monsters, they're just different kinds of magical creatures who can speak to you.

I think, however, she tends to be on the whole more serious about the Gothic than she is playful or critical. Think of the ongoing horror about Harry with his bloodline and what he might have inherited. Is he the heir of Slytherin? What does it mean that he can speak parseltongue?

And it's not just Harry, but the other characters as well. Remember Sirius Black's name, darkened off of his own family tree? That is a really powerful image. And I'm thinking, you know, as a Gothic reader, "What sort of bad blood is running through that family as well? What sins of the past are being revisited on the next generation? How much of fate is atoning for the evildoings of the past? How many basically old stories are going to be retold as echoes in a new generation?" That's just so Gothic.

I think we need to think, too, about the way Rowling deals with choice. The Gothic has traditionally been about characters who don't have much choice. One of the reasons the spaces are so claustrophobic and foreign and frightening is to show that the character is literally backed up against the wall. And so much of the series is about Harry learning what choices he does have in this narrow space that's been defined for him by prophesy, by other people's expectations, by his own hopes and what he's going to be in terms of growing from a boy to a man.

But there is a crucial moment in every book, and particularly of course in the last one, there are these crucial moments where he has to decide, well, as Dumbledore would say, "between what's right and what's easy" and using this genre seriously more than playfully, I think, to live in these confined spaces, whether it's miles underneath Hogwarts or underneath the stairs back with the Dursleys, to show that, yes, to some degree a lot of things have been decided for Harry, but in the end this is the story about the decisions that he gets to make himself. I think it's brilliant the way she does that and really underscores one of the main points of the entire series.

Travis: Well, we have to cut the conversation right there, it's all we have time for in this PotterCast segment. The rest of the conversation will be on another episode of Pottercast where we finish talking about Gothic elements of Harry Potter. Stay tuned, of course, for my HogsHead.org post later this week and at Pottercast.com and if you want more information about the Potter Pundits, visit us at PotterPundits. com.

CHAPTER 4

Gothic Schoolboy, Part 2

with Dr. Amy H. Sturgis

How Harry Potter Differs from Tom Brown and Billy Bunting and What He Has in Common with Frankenstein and Dracula

TRAVIS PRINZI: WELCOME TO another segment of Potter Pundits. This is Travis Prinzi, here to introduce you to the second part of a two part conversations we had on Gothic elements in Harry Potter. The first part was included in Pottercast 206. It's Halloween time, and it's time to talk about scary stories. This part of our talk explores more of the Gothic themes that pervade Harry Potter, but in it we also talk about other great Gothic writers; Ann Radcliffe, Edgar Allen Poe and H.P. Lovecraft, for example. Great literature reminds you of other great literature, and throughout this conversation, Harry Potter kept reminding us of other Gothic stories we'd read. Take these as recommendations for further reading in Gothic literature.

Here, then, are Potter Pundits, John Granger, author of *The Deathly Hallows Lectures*, James W. Thomas, author of *Repotting Harry Potter*, fantasy and science fiction scholar, Amy H. Sturgis, and myself, Travis Prinzi, author of *Harry Potter and Imagination*.

For more information on the Potter Pundits, please visit us – we created an information site, potterpundits.com just to learn more about us, and we'll be posting some additional information there for those interested in learning more about Gothic literature. And stay tuned, of course, to Pottercast.com where all the action is, where I'll be posting more later this week.

We pick up the conversation continuing the discussion of which Gothic elements in Harry Potter are meant to be just parody and where Gothic elements are meant to be taken much more seriously. We hope you enjoy this, and look forward to further conversation with you at PotterCast.

John: When Amy said it's not like Austen, there's at least one point where she does a real hat tip to the scene in *Northanger Abbey* where Moreland finds in her Gothic manor late at night what seems to be secret handwriting, she ctan barely sleep, she wants to know what this thing is...

Amy: [laughter] Right...

John: Amy starts to laugh because what this dangerous document turns out to be, in the morning, is a laundry list. But that whole book is largely an echo of Radcliffe's *Romance of the Forest* and she hat tips it all through *Abbey* and yet you'll get this playful mockery about it. We see that same sort of thing in *Prisoner of Azkaban* when we see the Grim, when Harry sees this big, black dog that's a death omen. And all through the book we get this, what in a Gothic novel would be this death omen, this horrible thing, and of course it turns out to be his godfather...

James: …we get a heavy dose of it every time we go to Divination class, too. Trelawney is the embodiment of the mockery of it all.

Travis: Is *Prisoner* also the book where he's sorting through the death omen books in Flourish & Blotts and comes across *Broken Balls: When Fortunes Turn Foul*? Did I get that right?

James: Yeah…

Travis: …so there's some humor going on there.

Now Amy said in her introductory material that Gothic literature becomes popular during times of social upheaval. Do we see that happening with Harry Potter?

(Silence, then laughter)

"Who wants to start?", I guess, is the question. John?

John: Is anything stable about the post-modern world? This is obviously an unstable time and our entertainment culture is permeated with the Gothic. This is just what you'd expect based on what Amy said. You turn on the television, and it's Buffy, and you look at the bookshelf and you've got Harry Potter and Twilight selling more than anything else. We have all sorts of para-normal Gothic fiction really taking the forefront at a time when people do feel terror. Not horror necessarily, but just the uncanny feeling that things aren't stable and that there's something just around the corner that's very dangerous.

Amy: In terms of the power dynamic, the way Ms. Rowling sets up the idea that there are people who haven't been represented, who haven't been treated right, who are in these positions of powerlessness.

- It's the Lupins of the world who are having to deal with all the regulations, and prejudices about werewolves,
- It's people like, well, the giants who have been driven off of their land and almost driven to extinction,

- Think about the way the goblins have been treated,
- And, of course, the way that the house elves have been treated.

Certainly, the reoccurring image is of the disenfranchised, even the people that Harry chooses to befriend, you know the mudbloods and the Weasleys, the mudblood lovers, right?

Look at all of these characters and what she's saying about groups that have been disenfranchised in one way or another. We know that she's worked with organizations that have dealt with prisoners of conscience and to serve people whose civil liberties have been abused in one way or another. It's no surprise, then, to see how she's painted the Ministry of Magic (I always like to point out you've got the Big Brother motif from *1984* and here you've got the big M.O.M., the Ministry of Magic). She's saying a lot of things about our times today and the things that bother her about our times.

She seems to think we're in a time of social upheaval as well, but also, to turn that around, a time of upheaval can also be a time of tremendous opportunity to do something about it.

Travis: And I wonder about something, especially as you're thinking about the timeline of the books. You've got four *Potter* books just came flying out up until 2000 when *Goblet* is published. And then you've got 2001 when September 11 happened. We then have a more than two year period with no *Potter* books, and then you have the darkest book by far of the series, *Order of the Phoenix*. We know alchemically as the *nigredo* that *Phoenix* had to be dark but I wonder how much influence the sudden change in the world political situation after 9/11 had on the portrayal of the Ministry in *Phoenix* and the constant fear that was gathering with very few really knowing how deep that fear and danger actually was...

John: I think you put your finger on it, Travis, about people's experience of the Ministry and Voldemort in *Phoenix*. Before 2001, the man on the street never thought about Osama Bin Laden and Islamic terrorism. But after the attacks of September 11, the Voldemort and the Death Eaters in *Order of the Phoenix* seems to be cast in the terrorist role and the Ministry as bunglers and appeasers. We can't find the bad guys, we don't know where they are, and some people in the media and government are denying that the black hats are really as dangerous as they are. The filter on our perception of the books changed tremendously. The political allegory was Gothic because our lives suddenly seemed Gothic.

James: I think it's really significant that it is in the third book, the chapter in *Prisoner* with the *Broken Balls* book that you mention, Travis, that's where that unnamed store manager has a conversation with Harry because Harry can't stop looking at *Death Omens: What to Do When You Know the Worst Is Coming*. Well, it is coming. And I ask my students sometimes "How many ways can we find out how we might die this day just by tuning in Fox or CNN in the morning?" We brainstormed one day and said "What are some death omens? What are people's fears?" Some kids start terrorist attacks, WMD's, West Nile Virus, bird flu, of course now we could add swine flu and E. coli lettuce leaves, and lead in toys from China. It never ends. But it's also striking that everything we thought of collectively in class that day was *post* 2001.

John: You're right you could go on and on with that list…

James: Yeah, it's so much about fear. Terror and fear, and I don't know much about the interrelationship between the two, but a character's attitude toward death or something after death, pretty much defines what he will fear and to what extent he or she will fear something, I think, throughout the series.

Travis: Well the whole *Potter* story is essentially how two people think about death: how Voldemort responds to death and how Harry responds to death.

James: Exactly. You heard me say in Dallas towards the end of my talk, Travis, I was embarrassed, and I said I'm trying to convince people that these are wonderful literary works and all I can come up with is "they're for love and against fear."

(Laughter)

John: Bringing this back to Gothic formula, isn't Voldemort, in his reaction to death, the classic Victorian Gothic scientist that wants to overcome death by creating a creature that has no conscience? He is a 21st Century Mr. Hyde, he is Frankenstein's monster, he's this creature without conscience, again, like Count Dracula, basically he's the un-dead. Voldemort has his body and his mind, his reason, but, as Ann Tracey says, rationality is the last thing you want to depend on in a Gothic novel, because it's going to all come down to your conscience and your spirit. When you realize, as Drs. Jekyll and Frankenstein do eventually, that there's no life without that conscience or spirit, then you're going to have to kill this character, this un-dead Hyde or monster who has no conscience.

The *Potter* novels, as Travis said, are essentially Harry's pursuit of love and conscience and doing the hard right thing in contrast with Voldemort's choices to become a maker and worshipper of idols. The Dark Lord literally creates idols for immortality in his Horcruxes by injecting his soul fragments into material things. He's thinking, of course, that's going to make him live forever. He becomes the quintessential materialist, without conscience, who's murdering people right and left in order to create means to his own ego's immortality.

In terms of the Gothic touches in the book, Voldemort is clearly the Gothic masterpiece, in that he embodies so many of the Gothic traditions single handedly, and he acts as this foil to Harry. Harry and Voldemort, through their mind link, which is I think a Dracula reference, that Mina Harker drinks his blood and so they have this mind link between the Gothic heroine...

Travis: ...the scar and everything...

John: ...that's right, the scar on the forehead. But that link there is to say only one of these characters, as the prophecy says, can survive. You can't do both of these things. You can't choose to be a materialist and an idol worshipper and a murderer and *also* say God is love, I'm spirit and conscience, and I make the hard, right choices. I mean every reader really has to make a divide there. Are you Harry? Or are you with Voldemort? And the triumph and joy of the story, of course, is that we all recognize Harry is right and choose to be with Harry.

Amy: You know, mentioning that, you just made me think of something, if I could just throw it in here real quickly. Another notion of sort of mind control and possession, the same way that Harry was afraid of what Voldemort was able to accomplish against him is *Trilby*, which was George du Maurier's book in 1894 which was a huge hit. He was the father of the author of *Rebecca* and *The Birds*, Daphne du Maurier, whose works are modern day Gothic masterpieces. But *Trilby* is the story of a man who essentially controls the mind of a young woman. If you read *Trilby*, the title refers to the young woman. But the man, who is described in it, if you read his description, it's Snape. Svengali is this man's name. And the way Svengali is described, with the long, lanky, dark hair, black hair and the black eyes, deep set... If you read the description, it's Severus Snape, which is really interesting too, because there is a way she's inverting your expectations, again, just, again, there's a connection that struck me that I hadn't seen made before, that I think is really, I reread it recently and thought, "Oh my goodness, that's Severus Snape."

John: Snape may be the quintessential Gothic character in the books, in that he seems to be a cross between four or five Gothic anti-heroes. I mean, clearly, he's Heathcliffe from *Wuthering Heights* in terms of his relationship with Lily. There's this unrequited love that goes on forever and just makes him more and more bitter and angry. It's his love, it's "always," but it doesn't make Severus, like Heathcliff, any nicer of a guy; he's just a sadist in the classroom, he hates Harry, he expresses frustration, he's lived his whole life to save Harry and now Dumbledore is going to kill him. But this regret doesn't mean he's done hating Harry; you get the feeling he'd be the first in line, now that it's time to kill Harry, that he'll let him have it.

I think Severus is clearly a Gothic scientist also, an accomplished scientist, much like Frankenstein, much like Dracula. (Stoker's Count Dracula is an alchemist.) And when we first meet Snape in the dungeon classroom, this is not a Trelawney cartoon figure. This is a man who is able to stopper death. We find out later this guy isn't kidding, that he actually can deliver on these things he talked about in his subterranean dungeon where he works his miracles. He is a very serious scientist ...

James: ...very heavy strain of that in Hawthorne with Aylmer in *The Birthmark*, and his Rappacini in *Rappaccini's Daughter* and other scientist figures...

Amy: Yes...

Travis: Mmmm...

John: I think that's a big piece of the Gothic, that it's the Romantic reaction against soulless scientism at least, not science per se, but this idea that "we're going to create a world without conscience, without love, and that it's going to be a better place because we have better sanitation." "We're going to have immunizations and that's going to mean that we're better people." The Romantic and Gothic writers seem to be saying in response, "We want character, we want truth and goodness, and beauty, which things you're not going to be able to produce or manipulate materially, scientifically."

James: If you want a 14-line example of where you were just going, check out Poe's 'Sonnet: To Science.' With that misleading title it sounds like it's going to be a tribute. Science is a "vulture whose wings are dull realities."

John: James, you're the Poe guy. Can you say some things about "the pale blue eyes"? When we open up *Deathly Hallows* and Harry is on the bed and he sees that mirror fragment and there's a pale blue eye looking up at him, I thought, "O my goodness..."

James: You're thinking of 'The Tell-Tale Heart,' I take it, and the young man in it.

John: Right.

James: The old man and his eye.

John: Can you tell the story?

James: The eyes in Poe, *when* they're embodied, pun intended, in a beautiful woman, are often large, luminous orbs of dark hue, language like that, and the early 20th century Freudian critics would predictably have a field day with regard to the loss of his mother, who, in the only miniature painting of her that survives, her eyes are very, very large indeed. But the other uses of eyes and the obsession of trying not to be looked at, or to destroy an eye, these often in male figures, not necessarily evil male figures, sometimes like the old man, are quite innocent, kindly male figures, but the eye of the black cat that he cuts out just this sort of "don't look at me" because the narrator has all kinds of problems, shortcomings. Poe wouldn't use the word, but he's obsessed with his own sins and his stories say, consequently, "Take the eye away from me, don't look at me."

John: So the eye is conscience, you think?

James: Yeah. Yeah. Yeah. Very much so in those better known ones; Black Cat, Telltale Heart. It seems that that's one very likely interpretation of it. Which is usually not perceived at all by the narrator, but we assume designed by Poe. That gap between Poe and those increasingly unreliable and eventually deranged narrators is another subject entirely, but...

Amy, is that in the Gothic tradition? Is there much of that evolution in a narrator in a Gothic work that we're convinced that he's sane and under control initially, and then he falls apart before our very eyes? Because Poe does that a lot.

Travis: You want to talk about *Shadow over Innsmouth*, Amy, don't you?

Amy: (Laughter) That's exactly where I was going. That's appropriate, too, because H.P. Lovecraft was a student of and great admirer of Poe so that fits that he used that disintegrating narrator as well. Lovecraft was all about entropy, the idea that things were falling apart. He wrote about this really well by describing characters, entire families even, that had become disreputable, that had become warped, so the great qualities they had once had were gone and now they were basically demented in one way or another. The Gaunts in Harry Potter, Lord Voldemort's mother's family, are the perfect example of that.

But you also have characters who get into that, discover their background, *Shadow over Innsmouth* is the great example of this, where a character is sort of thrown into a mystery, and he seems perfectly sane, but the more he discovers about the horrors going around him, he discovers:

a) they're horrible,

b) that they're related to him in ways he didn't realize, would never have imagined, and

c) he's not going to be sane once he gets to the bottom of things.

In fact a lot of characters in Lovecraft's work choose to know, even if they realize that what they will discover will destroy them. They'd still rather know and be destroyed than be ignorant and fearful of the unknown.

Then there are other stories in which, and I'm thinking 'The Colour Out of Space' that Lovecraft wrote and of other authors that Lovecraft admired who were doing the same kind of thing at the time, where by the end of the story, you're really not certain if you've just been spun a really entertaining tale by a crazy person or if you've just been told a very factual tale by someone who is incredibly sane and you're probably going to lose your sanity when it really hits you what you've just been told.

Travis: And isn't this what Harry's experienced? This is the story of Books 5 and 6, right? I mean, Harry's battle all the way through book 5 is "Am I possessed by Voldemort? Am I going to end up like him?" All the way through *Phoenix* he's confused, and then what does Dumbledore do in *Prince*? Instead of keeping Harry from Voldemort, Albus corrects his mistake and spends all of Book 6 teaching Harry the whole Horcrux history. Here's the family history.

Then we find out in Book 7, "Oh, by the way, Harry, you're descended from the same line, the Peverells on down, as the Dark Lord" so the reality was there behind Harry's fears. Harry really was facing the history of the Voldemort family line and choosing the good instead of the dehumanized Voldemort path. It's the same sort of story.

James: And clearly wanting to know all along. Wanting to know.

John: Amy mentioned this earlier in her introduction to Gothic literature. This decay of aristocratic privilege and the rise of the bourgeoisie is a real Gothic signature. We see the 'decay and rise' conflict in the apposition of the Weasleys and the Malfoys.

The Weasleys who are kind of middle class, a family with a lot of kids -- I guess they're supposed to be an Irish Catholic family even though they're not Irish or Catholic. The Malfoys, on the other hand, are this family embodiment of *prima geniture*. They have this one child on which all their hopes rest and they're about wealth and prestige, and they're in decay, consequently. Their morality and their ethical character are somehow atrophying. They are a family that's in decline, if only because they only have one child.

Which brings us back to Merope Gaunt, and the whole Gaunt family saga, which, as Amy mentioned, is really Voldemort's origin story. The Gaunts are a direct allusion to Thackery's *Vanity Fair,* in which the House of Gaunt literally is the place where the family is cursed by a "dark mark" on their threshold and the mysterious "taint of blood," which in *Vanity Fair* brings the Gaunts down from great social heights. They're nobility in decline.[3]

It's not just this one family, of course. This is one pointer to the larger war and trend going on inside of the *Harry Potter* novels between the Death Eaters, who are these pureblood nutters desperately holding on to power, fighting off this vibrant new bunch of outsiders represented by the Weasleys, who, though they may be poor or even socially taboo as "blood traitors," are the future. The Weasleys and their friends are taking over. These Gryffindor types are on the rise, not the pure bloods. Again, Gothic to the core: ascendant merchant class, aristocracy in decline.

James: Now you've all reminded me of Faulkner, and the aristocracy in decline, and the Compson family and their...

Amy: Faulkner is a great southern Gothic author...

James: Oh absolutely. And there the intermarriage is so parallel with the mudbloods and purebloods and

3   http://www.hogwartsprofessor.com/the-house-of-gaunt-is-it-from-vanity-fair/

so forth that one drop of black blood is pretty much what *Absalom Absalom* is all about. Father's rejection of a wife and son because a very slight amount of black blood. Don't get me started on Faulkner, though. (Laughter)

John: How about I list Gothic clichés and you guys come up with this kind of connections to Potterworld and literature? How about "fragmentation and reunion" for starters?. All of the great Gothic stories feature break-ups and then a kind of miraculous end-of-story reunion where the Gothic heroine is rescued. I'll start this one while you think.

The saddest parts of the books are when the trio break up. Reason? Harry, Ron and Hermione aren't together because of the Firebolt, the Goblet, or the Locket. Fortunately, there's always the joyous make-up. Even if the joyous return in *Deathly Hallows* is not so joyous on Hermione's part, it's essential to the whole working of that book that Ron take off and come back newly illumined.

There's also Harry's several reunions with his parents. His parents *are* dead and Rowling tells us they're never coming back to life yet we get to see them in the Mirror of Erised, we get to meet them in the *Goblet* graveyard, and then Harry walks to his own death with Mom and Dad holding his hand. We have that Gothic touch.

Travis: How about the *Hallows* Epilogue as a re-union piece for our traveling to Hogwarts? Last time we see Hogwarts in *Deathly Hallows*, everything is falling apart. There's a big battle, we see the fall of the bad guy, and then 19 years later they're all back together, there's no war going on, and they're sending their kids off to Hogwarts. That qualifies as something of a joyous return after a dramatic battle.

John: Yeah. It has to end that way because otherwise our last look at Kings Cross Station is with this very Gothic baby struggling on the floor and screaming, an infant that cannot be helped. That mental picture to me is up there on the terror scale with Harry in the forest with Voldemort drinking unicorn blood.

Amy: Another 'fragmentation and reunion' example would be the Weasley family becoming whole again when Percy comes back into the fold. Before they have this tragic loss, they are once more the Weasley Union facing everything together, and I think that was so important. Because that Percy schism in their family lasted for a couple of books and you just felt that niggling at you that you had this family that had stood together against so much had been torn apart and the fact that they came together again when it mattered most, I think, is really important.

James: That's a beautiful touch, it really is. For whatever reason, Molly always has the same number of sons, just about, as Harry becomes a son, Percy has drifted away, when Percy comes back, Fred is gone soon thereafter.

John: People are telling me that Fred's death was the most horrible moment for them in *Deathly Hallows* and I was arguing that Dobby's death is the one that's the real tear jerker. I think the reason that Fred's death isn't that horrific for me is exactly this point -- that he is fighting side by side with Percy as he dies. That they're literally joking and laughing together in this common cause, you think, what could be a finer death for a Weasley? I'm tearing up just thinking about it. It doesn't at all strike me as equivalent to the horror of Dobby returning to the house of Malfoy. I mean Malfoy Manor being this place of bad faith, quite literally...

Travis: ...and his own slavery, after all...

John: ...right, and he comes back to the dungeon. Talk about a Gothic scene! The heroine is being tortured upstairs, Dobby appears literally with a light in the darkness. This is a great Gothic scene. And then, of course, Dobby takes a knife in the chest sacrificially and he dies with Harry's names on his lips. This is Ann Radcliffe plus! This is *The Castle* on steroids.

Amy: Oh...and can I have a delayed reaction moment going back to your question about Snape and the great Gothic bad guys? I was trying to mine another one in my slowly functioning gray matter here. The one that came out to me beside *Trilby,* was from *The Italian or the Confessional of the Black Penitents* by Ann Radcliffe, which is 1797. The great villain who you feel quite sympathetic for in the end although he's horrible, is Schedoni, and he's the kind of mysterious monk who is always in the background, and you know he's playing politics, he's playing one side against the other. You're never sure which side he's on. And he follows across the country, Ellena, who it seems he's, well, he's kidnapped her, he torments her, and in the end you realize he is going to save her life. And he ends up dead by the end. And he's this dark brooding figure that is incredibly frightening and incredibly astute in the way he plays characters off of each other. And his whole sort of transformation being about the protector of the heroine is an interesting thing, and certainly a protector who doesn't want to be a protector. But it struck me that Schedoni is a great villain of Ann Radcliffe's and he's got Snape written all over him.

John: That's great because that's much more a part of the story than the Heathcliffe angle, which we only find out at the very end of the books.

Travis: Look. We're an hour in to our Gothic conversation and we still haven't even mentioned Dementors. There are so many Gothic elements in this series like these wraiths that we haven't begun to discuss. What about pictures of dehumanization? What about horcruxes? I mean there's a history of Horcrux type devices in fantasy. Tolkien traces the history in *On Fairy Stories* from all the way back from the *Tale of Two Brothers,* the old Egyptian tale, to George MacDonald's *The Giant's Heart.* Then to Rowling, who

60 *Harry Potter Smart Talk*

does it blatantly, doesn't she, in the *Warlock's Hairy Heart?*

The Horcrux and *Hairy Heart* idea is that we can protect ourselves from being hurt by encasing what makes us human in something else. This is a very Gothic theme that we can get away from fear, we can get away from pain, we can get away from everything we normally experience by taking what is essential to our humanity and separating it from ourselves.

John: That *Hairy Heart* story is probably the most concentrated Gothic piece that she does.

Travis: Well, we talked about a lot of different stories today, a lot of literature, and it might be a little bit overwhelming to some readers. Why don't we have Amy give us here and the pundits out there listening a few reading assignments? What would you recommend, Amy, to someone wanting to get a little bit more familiar with Gothic literature, and to see how Rowling has borrowed and taken and transformed Gothic elements? Where would you send people to get this reading?

Amy: Well, some have already been mentioned. Certainly, Charlotte Bronte's *Jane Eyre* is a great one. That's the Victorian incarnation of the Gothic. Going back earlier, I think Mary Wollstonecraft Shelley's *Frankenstein* or her *The Last Man* are really great works. I would also suggest something which you can find online, Joseph Sheridan LeFanu's *Carmilla* which predated Bram Stoker's *Dracula* by a number of years, and is a fantastic vampire story about a young adolescent girl who is basically indentured by a vampire. Really, really good stuff.

Contemporary stuff, I don't think it gets better than Neil Gaiman's *The Graveyard Book*, which just won both the Newberry Award and the Hugo Award this past year, which is the way I am ending my class that I am currently teaching on the Gothic imagination. And certainly any of the old classics, *Melmoth the*

Wanderer, Vathek, The Monk, Mysteries of Udolpho, The Italian, all the way back to *The Castle of Otranto*, I know several of these are available actually free in audio book versions from Libervox.org as well as online texts from Project Guttenberg.

John: You didn't mention H.P. Lovecraft.

Amy: Oh that's just blanket Gothic or otherwise. Read yourself some H.P. Lovecraft. Good, good, good stuff.

Travis: Well, thank you all for coming with us. Great conversation and lots to think about.

Amy: Thanks so much for having me. It's been a pleasure for me to be a special guest with you gentlemen on PotterCast.

PART II PUNDITS WRITING

CHAPTER 5 --- TRAVIS PRINZI

Harry Potter for Real Life

The Value of Elves and Wizards

S IR JAMES DYSON, CREATOR of the Dyson vac-
uum cleaner, thinks *Harry Potter* is dangerous for
society. Reports the *Times Online*:

> The UK's culture of venerating arts over sci-
> ence is all wrong, says Dyson. Harry Potter is an
> evil influence, he says, and arty-tarty stuff con-
> sumes too much popular attention.

> Is Potter really malign? "Um, yes," he admits.
> "I don't like those sort of fantasy books. If chil-
> dren read and enjoy them, fine, I don't morally
> object. But I'd be more interested in more practi-
> cal elements of life and showing children what
> they can do, not what they can't." (Woods)

Likewise, Richard Dawkins is concerned that *Harry Potter* might teach kids to believe in fairies and neglect science:

> "The book I write next year will be a children's book on how to think about the world, science thinking contrasted with mythical thinking.

> "I haven't read Harry Potter, I have read Pullman who is the other leading children's author that one might mention and I love his books. I don't know what to think about magic and fairy tales."

> Prof Dawkins said he wanted to look at the effects of "bringing children up to believe in spells and wizards".

> "I think it is anti-scientific – whether that has a pernicious effect, I don't know." (Beckford and Khan)

And lest you fear I'm only picking on scientific and atheist types, here's a religious person with the same opinion, writing into the *Times-Mail* news:

> I recommend that people stop wasting their time reading fiction (lies) for entertainment, and that parents teach their children by good example to spend more time reading wholesome nonfiction with literary value (including the Bible) for education. ("Potter debate still brewing")

My goal in the following pages is to vindicate your love for *Harry Potter* (as if you need it!) by doing two things: Showing you the nature of imaginative fiction, and showing the practical applicability and value of imaginative fiction. In other words: I want to demonstrate why Dyson, Dawkins, and the nameless pundit above are wrong.

My story goes like this: I started out in college intent to pursue a degree in secondary English education. After two years of this, I got distracted by six years of theological studies. I learned in this process that parents often have really good advice: my dad told me to double major in theology and English education. I didn't listen, and I should have, because after those 6 years of theology, I returned to get an English education degree. I now have a Master's in both disciplines.

What got me back onto the English Ed track? Well, there's the very practical reason that there isn't much to do with a theology degree! But what really happened is that, while nearing the end of my M.A. in theological studies, I picked up *Harry Potter*. My love for literature, after six years of reading almost nothing but theologians, was reignited. The combination of these two disciplines and the brilliant professors who helped me achieve success in them gives me, if I may say so, a unique perspective on imaginative fiction in general and *Harry Potter* in specific. So I'll proceed with some observations about why *Harry Potter* deserves to be called great literature, and we'll see if you agree.

What are Great Books?

The Great Books of the Western World idea, first put forth by Mortimer Adler, has had a fascinating history, not without difficulty. As James W. Thomas has rightly put it, the canon for too long was dominated by "DWEM: dead, white, European males." This has been changing in recent years, and to borrow once again from Dr. Thomas, the Great Books canon is now much more of a loose canon.

This problem aside, the *idea* of a Great Books canon is not a bad one, and Adler gave three basic criteria for a Great Book. A "Great Book" is one that:

- has contemporary significance
- is inexhaustible - can be read over and over with benefit
- is relevant to a large number of the great ideas that have been addressed in literature over the past 25 centuries

I think *Harry Potter* fits these three criteria well. I'm going to take them in random order, because I want to spend the majority of time on numbers 1 and 3.

Harry Potter is Inexhaustible

On this point, number 2 above, I will be very brief. I recall giving a talk for kids at a local library on name meanings in Harry Potter. A few older folks showed up, one a bright college-age woman. I asked near the beginning how many times the kids had read the books. I heard a variety of expected answers: "two, four, five." The young woman then raised her hand and said, "Thirty-two." The number itself might not be as surprising as the fact that she actually kept count up through thirty-two!

It's hard to doubt that the *Potter* books are re-readable, but the question is *why*.

C.S. Lewis wrote:

> The re-reader is looking not for actual surprises (which can come only once) but for a certain surprisingness. [...] Knowing that the surprise is coming we can now fully relish the fact that this path through the shrubbery doesn't *look* as if it were suddenly going to bring us to the edge of the cliff. So in literature. Not till the curiosity, the sheer narrative lust, has been given its sop and laid asleep, are we at leisure to savour the real beauties. ("On Stories," 18)

Of course, if the surprises are all cheap thrills, and finding out what happened is the whole experience of the book, it's not a great book. That's why great ideas have to be attached to it. But re-reading Rowling provides treasure troves of "real beauties," to use Lewis's words. Exploring the series' symbolism, its alchemical scaffolding, its political satire, and the brilliant foreshadowing can keep a reader re-reading for thirty-two times and beyond.

As I'll assume that you who hold this book need not be convinced that *Harry Potter* merits re-reading and contains benefits with each re-read, let's move on to some of the "real beauties" contained within Rowling's stories.

Great Books are about Great Ideas

The past 25 centuries have contained a wide variety of literature, but the truly influential and lasting works have been the ones that have meaningfully addressed what J.R.R. Tolkien called "primordial human desires" ("On Fairy Stories"). In other words, Great Books teach us about humanity. Russell Kirk, author of fiction and political philosopher, wrote that "the end of great books is ethical - to teach us what it means to be genuinely human" ("The Moral Imagination"). Or to visit perhaps a more complex definition by Russell Kirk: Great Books are possessed of a "moral imagination," which is "that ethical perception that aspires to right order in the soul and right order in the commonwealth." Or to simplify once again: Great Books teach us what it means to be human, and how to live with other humans.

Well, this is a very complex matter, and no mistake. Undoubtedly, books will answer the great questions of humanity in different ways, and some authors will have different views than others on what the right questions are in the first place. But let's take three major ideas that almost all agree upon and see how *Harry Potter* addresses them. These ideas are:

- Life as a mystery
- Dealing with fear
- Sacrificial love

The three ideas go together, in fact. The first one is a given to all but the arrogant: there's a lot of stuff about being human that goes beyond the perception of the five senses and the experimentation of the scientific laboratory. None of us have it all figured out, and it's the mystery of life that drives us to stories. Contrary to popular opinion, we're not rushing to the bookshelf to escape reality, but to find corollaries to it - corollaries that help us make sense of life and learn how to live in this strange world.

The master of horror, H.P. Lovecraft, wrote, "The oldest and strongest emotion of mankind is fear, and the oldest and strongest kind of fear is fear of the unknown" ("Supernatural Horror in Literature"). This is precisely why our earliest stories, like "The Epic of Gilgamesh," were about death. What is more "unknown" and frightening than what happens after death?

This, then, is why we love both mystery/detective fiction and Gothic literature. They both deal with the unknown, one usually having to do with solving a murder (a metaphorical conquering of death's mystery) and the other with supernatural terror related to death. J.K. Rowling, expert genre-blender, easily melds these two types of literature into her *Harry Potter* stories. We can see this symbolized in the mysterious death discussed at the beginning of *Half-Blood Prince*.

> "But that murder was in the newspapers," said the Prime Minister, momentarily diverted from his anger. "Our newspapers. Amelia Bones... it just said she was a middle-aged woman who lived alone. It was a--a nasty killing, wasn't it? It's had rather a lot of publicity. The police are baffled, you see."

> Fudge sighed. "Well, of course they are," he said. "Killed in a room that was locked from the inside, wasn't she? We, on the other hand, know exactly who did it, not that that gets us any further toward catching him. (HBP-1)

It's a fun conversation if you know your Edgar Allen Poe. Poe was famous for his Gothic literature, but he also wrote one of the first ever detective stories: "The Murder in Rue Morgue," which concerns the same type of case - a murder in a room locked from the inside. In Poe's "Muggle" world, the explanation had to do with a gorilla and a window lock that didn't work properly. In the Wizarding World, it's much easier to solve: the murdered Apparated into the room, killed the victim, and Apparated back out. Case solved.

The *Harry Potter* books are both detective novels and Gothic literature.

Sherlock Harry

Each *Harry Potter* novel is a detective book. There's a mystery to each one. In *Philosopher's Stone*, it's the mysterious hidden object and the identity of Nicholas Flamel. In *Chamber of Secrets*, it's the mysterious writings on the wall and voices in the walls. In *Prisoner of Azkaban*, it's the identity and whereabouts of Sirius Black, and more importantly, why he would want to kill Harry. In *Goblet of Fire*, it's the culprit who entered Harry into the Triwizard Tournament. In *Order of the Phoenix*, it's the weapon Voldemort seeks. In *Half-Blood Prince*, it's the identity of the title character whose name Harry finds on his potions book. In *Deathly Hallows*, it's the three Hallows themselves, and the whereabouts of the Horcruxes.

So Harry Potter, that magical sleuth extraordinaire, spends book after book getting it completely wrong. Snape is not trying to steal the stone. Draco is not the heir of Slytherin. Sirius Black does not want to kill him. It was not Karkarov who put his name in the Goblet. Sirius was not being tortured by Voldemort in the Ministry. The Half-Blood Prince was not his dad. And the Hallows were not a good idea for a distraction from the Horcrux hunt.

Ah, but those Hallows! That's where Harry finally begins to get it right - when standing in Dobby's grave, he finally gives up his arrogant need to know, and chooses instead to humbly believe.

And by believing, he finally knows.

This knowledge increases one step at a time. Horcruxes, not Hallows. Check. The location of the final Horcruxes, Check. Oops - one more: I'm a Horcrux. Check. Snape loved mom. Check. I gotta go die now. Check.

He accepts each bit of knowledge and responds to it properly. He navigates each situation and makes the difficult choice. And then he finally meets his maker.

Or maybe just Dumbledore. But they're almost the same thing. Dumbledore, the god-like figure, upon whom doubt has been cast, but in whom Harry has placed his trust, reveals the whole plan, repents his secrecy from Harry, and sends him back to finish the quest. It was all Dumbledore's sovereign plan the whole time.

After *Deathly Hallows* was released, one blogger started referring to Dumbledore as Rat!Bastard Dumbledore. Mind your language! We need not come down so hard on Dumbledore for orchestrating this master plan. Harry *had to die.* Had to. No question about it. As long as Harry lives, Voldemort lives. But let's remember that Dumbledore didn't make Harry a Horcrux. Dumbledore didn't create the weapon that would one day defeat Voldemort; Voldemort went ahead and did that himself, by acting on partial knowledge.

All Dumbledore had to do was figure out what to do with the knowledge of the scarcrux. We may not like his choice, but one thing is certain: Dumbledore was pretty sure Harry was going to make it through this thing all right. Remember that "gleam of triumph" at the end of *Goblet of Fire?* That's Dumbledore's realization that Harry no longer had to die; or at least, he no longer had to *stay dead*. The twin connection Voldemort created with Harry's blood would make it possible for Harry to return to life after getting zapped by the green light of death.

So Harry returns, having heard the whole story, and something incredibly odd happens: Harry suddenly knows more than even the reader knows. He's the master of the Elder Wand.

What?

This is one of those moments in the series where you had to go back and re-read it a few times to figure out what had just happened. Basically, it's this: Because Harry wrestled a wand that was not the Elder Wand away from Draco, who was unwittingly master of the Elder Wand because he disarmed its true master (somehow the wand, though it never actually "met" Draco, chose him anyway), he was now master of the Elder Wand which Draco never knew he was master of and which had passed its allegiance from Dumbledore to Draco to Harry, so that - surprise! - the wand Voldemort was holding was not going to kill its true master, Harry.

Got that?

OK, assuming that (a) no one overpowered Draco in any way, shape, or form from the time he disarmed Dumbledore, and (b) in the half-century since Dumbledore had defeated Grindelwald, not single person - not one! - had disarmed Dumbledore or overpowered him in any way, shape or form, then perhaps we can let Rowling off on the technicality. Wand lore is tricky business, after all. And Rowling's answer for why she planned the transfer as such a trivial act is more than satisfactory, and really quite pleasing:

> I said to Arthur, my American editor – we had an interesting conversation during the editing of seven – the moment when Harry takes Draco's wand, Arthur said, God, that's the moment when the ownership of the Elder wand is actually transferred? And I said, that's right. He said, shouldn't that be a bit more dramatic? And I said, no, not at all, the reverse. I said to Arthur, I think it really puts the elaborate, grandiose plans of Dumbledore and Voldemort in their place. That actually the history of the wizarding world hinged on two teenage boys wrestling with each other. They weren't even using magic. It became an ugly little corner tussle for the possession of wands. And I really liked that – that very human moment, as opposed to these two wizards who were twitching strings and manipulating and implanting information and husbanding information and guarding information, you know? (Anelli, "Vault #10")

A good answer, packed with meaning which there's no space here to unpack.

Harry's knowledge of the flaw in the plan is much like Sherlock Holmes, who possesses abilities of insight that the rest of us do not. You know the formula. Distraught person shows up at Sherlock's door. Sherlock, who happens to be entertaining Watson at the time, listens to the story of Distraught Person, and that person then leaves. Watson exclaims that Distraught Person has, indeed, come with a very mysterious issue, to which Sherlock responds something to the effect of: "My dear Watson, if you just looked at her boots, and the stains on left sleeve, and the way her right pinky fingernail was chipped, and the three strands of her hair that hung down in front of her face, then you'd know that it was Mr. Plum in the kitchen with a revolver." Or something like that.

When Harry reveals the flaw in the plan, he's unveiling the mystery for everyone involved. I dare say no readers had worked it out that Harry's stealing of Draco's blackthorn wand resulted in his becoming master of the Elder Wand.

Harry's Gothic Journey: Dealing with Death

Harry makes his way through Gothic structures during the seven books. Another chapter of this book deals with Gothic issues in detail, but for now, let's consider Harry's developments through Books 5-7.[4] In Book 5, Harry deals with the most tragic experience he consciously remembers: Sirius's death. He doesn't respond well. In his greatest moment of grief to date, Harry yells at Dumbledore: "THEN - I DON'T - WANT - TO - BE - HUMAN!" This is a scary moment for Harry, because this is Voldemort's own wish. He rejects humanity in order to preserve biological life and avoid pain. Harry is willing to reject his humanity to avoid pain as well. The hero has reached a crisis point, completely torn down, and seems to want to give up humanity, to become something non-human, to escape hurting. As I argue in chapter four of *Harry Potter & Imagination*, the best definition of evil in the Harry Potter series is dehumanization. Harry seems ready to embrace evil in this moment.

This is why Dumbledore's lessons with Harry in *Half-Blood Prince* were so important - and so very Gothic. His first lesson with Dumbledore is a trip

---

4   Which also happen to be overarching set-up for the alchemical work: Black (Book 5), White (Book 6), Red (Book 7).

into the Pensieve which results in observing the distorted humanity of the Gaunts. The scene is filled with a combination of the Gothic and the grotesque: "large amounts of ... yellow pus," which "flowed" from Bob Ogden's nose, blood, filth, pale faces, dead snakes, "muck," Merope's "flushing blotchily scarlet," spit, and other pointers to gross distortions of humanity; much of the scene takes place inside the filthy Gaunt house. Where does Harry end his journey of book 6? With a trip into a cave filled with Gothic imagery (Inferi!), in which Harry finally begins to emerge as Dumbledore's successor. Harry's development under Dumbledore into a hero is framed in Gothic imagery. Through it all, Dumbledore is building to a key point, which he had rejected at the end of the previous year: Love (which leads to grief) is Harry's greatest asset, the "power the Dark Lord knows not."

Love Understood in the Grave of an Elf

At the end of the sixth book, Harry still doesn't get Dumbledore's lesson about love. It doesn't make sense to him until he's standing in Dobby's grave. Even at his own parents' graves, he doesn't believe in love's victory over death, and even wishes to be buried with them. But when he digs Dobby's grave, it finally begins to sink in.

Dobby's death is consistently the toughest moment in the series for me. I remember well the release night for *Deathly Hallows*. I went to the store to pick up two copies - one for me and one for my wife. I got home, and she had spread out bowls of candy all over the bed. We were going to stay up reading, and we were going to need sugar. I got ahead of her in the reading, and in the wee hours of the morning came upon the scene where Dobby died. I slammed the book, got up, and walked away. My wife was concerned!

And it gets worse with each reading. I remember listening to the audiobook while raking leaves in my backyard. In the middle of my yard work, I reached the point of Dobby's death, and there I was, standing in the middle of my yard, tears streaming down my face. Why is this such a difficult moment for us, and such a transformative one for Harry? Because Dobby clearly *loves* Harry. And not only that, but Dobby loves Harry *freely*. "Here lies Dobby, a free elf," Harry writes on his tombstone.

The quest to bring down Voldemort would have failed. They were all trapped in Malfoy Manor, and Voldemort was on his way. Had Dobby not showed up and willingly given his life, it would have all been over. For the first time, it really sunk in how sacrificial love that defeats death and evil. Harry saw it, experienced it, and began to believe in Dumbledore's plan.

Remember that at this beginning of this quick survey of Harry's Gothic journey, we were discussing Sirius's death. It was in Harry's conversation with Dumbledore that the latter pressed the point about Sirius's treatment of Kreacher playing a role in Sirius's eventual death. On either sides of this journey, then, we have a house-elf: one who, out of anger at being mistreated, caused the death of another, and one who, out of love and freedom, gives up his life to save other lives.

All of this is done by imaginary elves, and somehow, we are affected. And that leads us to ask why.

Harry Potter's Ongoing Contemporary Significance: A Path to a Brighter Future

To some extent, it's cheating to take Mortimer Adler's first point - a Great Book "has contemporary significance" - of a current novel. Of *course* it has contemporary significance; it's a contemporary book! But I think we can fairly argue that Rowling's books will continue to hold significance, because she is dealing with classical themes of humanity and bringing them into the postmodern world.

This is precisely why S.P.E.W. fails. S.P.E.W. is a contemporary, postmodern method of dealing with the concerns of justice and equality: self-righteous social crusade. After *Deathly Hallows* was released, one essayist wrote the following, in complaint:

> And then there is the hope for the "And Justice for All" ending (or at least a path to a brighter future). It died! It died when Grawp was given no leadership role within the population of Giants. It died when Remus was killed and left Fenrir as the werewolf leader. And it died when Bellatix's knife killed Dobby. And this was the cruelest blow of all. Dobby had been, for us, the symbol of potential freedom for the house elves and others. Dobby died and with him the hope for a bright and shining future for all died with him.

Here is someone who very much missed the point of the *Harry Potter* books. If you've gotten to the end of all seven books, and you conclude that someone's death can't change the world for the better and create a "path to a brighter future," then you're in serious need of a re-read! Dobby's death is precisely what will create a brighter path to the future.

Dobby's situation is representative of the key contemporary social issue addressed in the *Potter* books: racism. Muggles oppressed magical folk, driving them into hiding. Purebloods oppress Muggleborns. The Wizarding community oppresses other magical brethren - house-elves, centaurs, giants and goblins. It's an ugly situation all around. S.P.E.W. is the usual response to injustice: if we shout and protest loudly enough, we can change the world.

J.K. Rowling pushes us in another direction. At the 2008 Harvard commencement speech, she quoted Plutarch: "What we achieve inwardly will change outer reality." This is why self-sacrificial love is the real heart of the books and their social message. No one leads the house-elves to freedom by the end of Book 7. The giants and centaurs do not re-integrate with society. Goblins are not permitted wands simply because Harry Potter defeated Voldemort. But she has given us a "path to a brighter future."

How? One can imagine that Harry will spread Dobby's story far and wide. Dobby told Harry in *Chamber of Secrets* that Harry was a hero to house-elves, because his victory over Voldemort as an infant led to better conditions for their kind. Harry represented a "new dawn" for the house-elves. What do you imagine house-elves will say when they learn that Harry's second and final victory over Voldemort was accomplished because of the courageous work of Dobby, "a free elf"? If the house-elves have learned to love their slavery because they've been forced into it and told lies about themselves for thousands of years, it will take a significant event to begin to break them of their psychological slavery. Dobby's sacrificial death might just be the start of that process.

This is where the *Harry Potter* books are particularly significant on the moral/allegorical level. You've never met a house-elf, but somehow, you care about their plight. With me, you find yourself feeling a bit foolish as tears stream down your face because an imaginary elf died. But you and I have no need to be concerned about our mental and emotional health; our response to the death of Dobby is quite human. Rowling told the 2008 Harvard grads:

> Unlike any other creature on this planet, humans can learn and understand, without having experienced. They can think themselves into other people's places.

This unique gift to humanity is, Rowling argues through her stories, the imaginative key to working for justice in the world. If we can remember what it's like to feel and to hurt for other people by feeling and hurting for house-elves, we can then return to our own primary world and do the same. We can think ourselves into the place of those who are treated unjustly and imagine and work for a better world.

If Great Books and imaginative fiction do indeed matter to society, and if *Harry Potter* fits the description of a great work of imaginative literature, then Sir James Dyson and Richard Dawkins have no need to be concerned about its influence. John Ruskin said it well:

> It is quite an inexorable law of this poor human nature of ours, that in the development of its healthy infancy, it is put by Heaven under the absolute necessity of using its imagination as well as its lungs and its legs;- that it is forced to develop its power of invention, as a bird its feathers of flight.

Imagination is directly related to invention, because it's in the exercise of the imagination that we learn and believe in the value of life. The mythic meaning leads us to the scientific discovery. Nothing in a scientific laboratory teaches us that there are things worth dying for, and that fear can be overcome by willing self-sacrifice.

We learn those things, oddly enough, from elves and wizards.

Bibliography

Beckford, Martin and Urmee Khan, "Harry Potter fails to cast spell over Richard Dawkins." *Telegraph*. October 24, 2008. http://www.telegraph.co.uk/news/3255972/Harry-Potter-fails-to-cast-spell-over-Professor-Richard-Dawkins.html

Kirk, Russell. "The Moral Imagination." *Literature and Belief Vol. 1* (1981), 37–49. Also published in Reclaiming a Patrimony (Washington, DC: The Heritage Foundation, 1982), 45–58. Reproduced at *The Russell Kirk Center for Cultural Renewal*. http://www.kirkcenter.org/index.php/detail/the-moral-imagination/

Lewis, C.S. *Of Other Worlds*. San Diego: Harper Inc, 1966, p. 18.

"Potter debate still brewing." *Times-Mail News*. 3 August 2007. 23 August 2007.

Rowling, J.K. *Harry Potter and the Chamber of Secrets*. New York: Scholastic, Inc., 1999.

Rowling, J.K. *Harry Potter and the Deathly Hallows*. New York: Scholastic, 2007.

Rowling, J.K. *Harry Potter and the Goblet of Fire*. New York: Scholastic, Inc., 2000.

Rowling, J.K. *Harry Potter and the Half-Blood Prince.* New York, Scholastic Inc., 2005.

Rowling, J.K. *Harry Potter and the Order of the Phoenix.* New York: Scholastic, Inc., 2003.

Rowling, J.K. *Harry Potter and the Sorcerer's Stone.* New York: Scholastic, Inc., 1997.

Rowling, J.K. "The Fringe Benefits of Failure, and the Importance of Imagination." *Harvard University Gazette Online.* http://www.news.harvard.edu/gazette/2008/06.05/99-rowlingspeech.html.

Ruskin, John. *The Art of England: Lectures Given at Oxford.* Google Books.

Tolkien, J.R.R. "On Fairy-Stories" in *Tales from the Perilous Realm.* Boston: Houghton Mifflin Harcourt, 2008.

Woods, Richard. "Buzz off, Harry Potter - we need reinventing." *Times Online.* May 9, 2010. http://business.timesonline.co.uk/tol/business/industry_sectors/engineering/article7120489.ece

CHAPTER 6 --- J A M E S T H O M A S

Mystery, Magic, and Music

Harry Potter's Journey From "Interesting Uncertainty"
to "Incomprehensible Certainty" and Beyond

I N J. K. R O W L I N G's *Harry Potter and the Half-Blood Prince*, as Dumbledore is trying to find the place where he and Harry may pass through the cave wall, the wisest of wizards is "simply . . . looking and touching" (558).⁵ Harry is not surprised at this low-key magic since he has "long since learned that bangs and smoke were more often the marks of ineptitude than expertise." I believe that we initially enjoy the Rowling books because of the bangs and smoke and that later, as re-readers, we appreciate them for the looking and the touching. Moreover, in *Harry Potter and the Order of the Phoenix*, Dumbledore apologetically tells Harry that he has lately forgotten "what it was to be young" (826). The Potter books would seem to be for the young and, to use Yeats's wonderful phrase, to be "no country for old men."⁶

---

5   *Page references are to the American editions of the Potter books and will be cited parenthetically.*
6   *This is the opening line of William Butler Yeats's "Sailing to Byzantium."*

Yet there are times, as when readers encounter many of Dumbledore's words of wit and wisdom in all seven books, when even the most precocious and wisest of children, eager to solve the most intriguing of mysteries, could not possibly fathom the depth and the mysteries of the headmaster's words. Harry's saga *is* a country for men and women much older than Harry, Ron, Hermione, and many of their friends and enemies.

Certainly, the enormously popular Harry Potter books are, among many other things, excellent detective fiction. As many have noted, in Rowling's Harry, Ron, and Hermione, readers get the Hardy boys and Nancy Drew together solving mysteries aplenty. Each of the seven novels poses questions to be answered and good, old-fashioned mysteries to be solved. Where is the sorcerer's stone? Who has opened the Chamber of Secrets? Where is Sirius Black, the escaped prisoner? Who put Harry's name in the Goblet of Fire? Can the Order of the Phoenix defeat Lord Voldemort? Who is the Half-Blood Prince? Where in the world are the dreaded Horcruxes?

Rowling's deceptively complex novels, however, should be considered mysteries in a far different sense as well. Gerard Manley Hopkins described his faith journey as moving from seeing mystery as "interesting uncertainty" to seeing it as "incomprehensible certainty."[7] This seems descriptive of the evolution Rowling's Harry undergoes in his seven-part saga. The mysteries, the uncertainties, that Harry initially solves are indeed "interesting"; often they are compelling and extremely dangerous. Yet these mysteries are solvable and solved. By the final book in the series, however, the mystery that Harry confronts and seeks

---

7   *Letter, Gerard Manley Hopkins to Robert Bridges, October 24,* 1883.

to resolve is a certainty: he must die so that evil will be defeated and so that those whom he loves might live. Though these things are certain, the overall plan remains incomprehensible to Harry and to us, along with many other incomprehensible certainties Harry encounters and ponders.

The first of these kinds of mystery I would like to focus on is the mystery of faith. Faith in the Potter books has its polar opposites in Hermione, the rational skeptic who, arguably, tends to believe in too little too late, and Luna Lovegood, who believes in too much, much too soon. Yet, in the end, both have complete faith in Harry and the truth. In *Deathly Hallows* we have a discussion of whether or not "The Tale of the Three Brothers" is true. The dialogue between Hermione and Luna's father Xenophilius is essentially a discussion of faith. Xeno probably believes more things based on less evidence than most of us do, and Hermione seems to believe less than most of us without hard evidence. He may believe in Crumple-Horned Snorkacks, which he has never seen and which do not exist; but he also believes in the three Hallows, which he has not seen and which do exist. Hermione believes in neither until she sees the Hallows for herself. Here and countless other times in the Potter books, Rowling gives readers examples of people having faith in things unseen, things about which they are certain yet which they cannot fully comprehend, reminding us of *Mysterium Fidei*, the mystery of faith.

Arguably the most famous example may be when Harry asks Dumbledore in the King's Cross scene in the final book, "Is this real or has this been happening inside my head?" and the headmaster answers, "Of course it is happening inside your head, Harry, but why on earth should that mean that it is not real?"

(723). Harry's wanting to know if "this" is "real" or
not is tantamount to wanting to see clearly what, as St.
Paul says, humans can now only see "through a glass
in a dark manner" (I Corinthians 13:12) and is reminiscent of the definition of "faith" as "the evidence of
things that appear not" (Hebrews 11:1).[8]

Rowling's Dumbledore also seems to attempt to
address the mystery of death. From the first book to
the last his not fearing death and its mysteries is in
contrast to Voldemort's concept of conquering death
by attempting to live on and on in an unnatural state
by severing his soul. Dumbledore tells Harry in Book
1 that "to the well-organized mind, death is but the
next great adventure" (297); in Book 6, he says, "It is
the unknown we fear when we look upon death and
darkness, nothing more" (566); and in the final book
Dumbledore says of Voldemort, "He fears the dead.
He does not love" (721). Dumbledore has a wonderful
conversation with Harry in *Prisoner of Azkaban* when
Harry, confused and embarrassed, talks of thinking
he had seen his dead father. "You think the dead we
loved ever truly leave us?" Dumbledore asks him (427).

Rowling would seem to be answering the headmaster's question throughout the novels—from her choice
of an epigraph for the final book (a passage from
William Penn on the subject the beloved ones we lose
to death paradoxically being present with us still) to
her invention of thestrals.

These are creatures that can only be seen by those
who have seen someone die, as Harry and Luna have;
they are memento mori creatures, in essence. Harry,
with Hagrid's instruction and Luna's example, learns
that thestrals are not horrible creatures (the way those
who cannot see them think of them), but they are

---

8   Biblical quotations are to the Douay Rheims Version.

beautiful animals not to be feared, dreaded, or avoid-
ed once we know how to look at them, once we can
see them. These veiled observations about death and
those who have seen it are quite unforgettable—perhaps especially to those of us, and I am one, who can
see thestrals. Later in Book 5, Luna tells Harry that
she is certain she will see her dead mother again, and
is in "disbelief" over Harry's uncertainty about this
incomprehensible matter (863).

Following their extraordinary conversation, Harry
feels less pain about the death of his godfather and is
a bit more enlightened about this mystery, ironically
by a wonderful young lady most of the other students
call "Loony."

Rowling's shortest chapter in all 4100 pages of
Harry's story is the graveyard scene in *Goblet of Fire*
wherein Lord Voldemort returns to bodily form and
to power. The scene is rich in its implications about
the mysteries of death and resurrection; it is a parody
of incarnation and a kind of reverse resurrection. We
witness in the scene not the holy birth of a child in a
manger, but the unholy rebirth of a man in a cauldron.
Moreover, the chant just before Voldemort rises contains the work *"resurrect"* (642). Christians affirm that
Christ in bodily form died and rose again so that *souls*
could live. Voldemort is now born again to work evil
in the world, having split his soul so he can live on in
his *body*.

In the final book of the series, Harry finds his parents' gravesite and reads the inscription on the stone.
It is from I Corinthians 15:26: *"The last enemy that
shall be destroyed is death"* (328). Harry, never having
read the passage, is disturbed, thinking it contains a
Voldemort-like idea, wishing to conquer death and live
on in body. Hermione explains the mystery to Harry,

who learns that St. Paul's words mean "living beyond death. Living after death," and, once again, Harry is confronted with an incomprehensible certainty.

Appropriately, a few verses after the quoted verse on the tombstone, St. Paul writes to the Corinthians: "Behold, I tell you a mystery" (I Corinthians 15:51).

Throughout the Potter books, we find occasional references to a department at the Ministry of Magic, located on the lowest level and known as the Department of Mysteries. Here workers, known as Unspeakables, study what Steve Vander Ark has called "some of the deepest mysteries of existence" (*The Lexicon* 216). In *Order of the Phoenix*, Harry and five of his friends enter this mysterious place where mysteries are pondered, passing through three doors leading to areas where thought, death, and time are studied—finding there, among other things, human brains, a mysterious veil through which the living pass to another realm, and a bell jar wherein a hummingbird emerges from its egg, ages, returns to its egg, and hatches again. Wondrous as all these mysteries are, Harry and his friends cannot pass through one door in the Department of Mysteries; the charm magic folk use to open locked doors does not work, and Harry's magic knife supposedly able to open any door is melted in the attempt to open this one. The implications are rich indeed since Harry does enter the places where thought, death, and time are pondered, but cannot enter the room where, it turns out later, Unspeakables study the mystery of love. Love defies thought, goes on after death, and, as Shakespeare says "is not Time's fool"; the place where it is studied is the hardest door to open.

Dumbledore later explains to Harry that this room in the Department of Mysteries that is always locked contains "a force that is at once more wonderful and more terrible than death, than human intelligence, than forces of nature" (843). He adds that this force is "the most mysterious of the many subjects for study that reside there" and that Harry possesses it in great quantities while Voldemort has it "not at all" (844-45). In Book 6 this "force," though implicit here, Dumbledore identifies explicitly as love—"just love"; this is the "power" identified in a prophecy about Harry, and it is the "power the Dark Lord knows not" (509). Dumbledore's paradoxical use of both "wonderful" and "terrible" to describe love is reminiscent of one of the central paradoxes in Keirkegaard's *Fear and Trembling*: that to be human is both a terrible and a wonderful thing.

Not only does Harry come to love unconditionally and sacrificially as his saga unfolds, he is protected from the beginning because of his mother's love and her dying for him. As Dumbledore explains to Harry in Book 1, Lily's death to save her son is what has protected and will protect him from the Dark Lord: "to have been loved so deeply, even though the person who loved us is gone, will give us some protection forever. It is in your very skin" (299). Hundreds of pages later, in Book 5, Dumbledore reminds Harry that he is "protected by an ancient magic" and that his mother's sacrifice "gave you a lingering protection . . . that flows in your veins to this day" (835-36). Writing in *Looking for God in Harry Potter*, John Granger affirms: "If there is a single meaning to the Potter books . . . it is that love conquers all. And of all loves, sacrificial love is the most important, because it has conquered death" (124); Granger's observation was written, incidentally, before Books 6 and 7 were published.

Countless times in the Potter books Dumbledore reminds Harry how extraordinary he is since he possesses such a deep and profound "force" or "power" as love, and, conversely, those who cannot love and know not its power, stand in stark contrast or even mock him. In the shack scene in *Prisoner of Azkaban*, Peter Pettigrew seems to think his treachery that resulted in Harry's parents' death is justified because otherwise Voldemort "would have killed me" (375). Sirius's shouted response is "THEN YOU SHOULD HAVE DIED! . . . DIED RATHER THAN BETRAY YOUR FRIENDS, AS WE WOULD HAVE DONE FOR YOU!" Indeed, this is descriptive of what virtually every person in the shack except Peter would have done, and will be willing to do, for each other in future years.

This is obviously reminiscent of "Greater love than this no man hath, that a man lay down his life for his friends" (John 15:13). Harry surely will long recall what his godfather Sirius says in the shack; and Sirius will die helping to defend Harry, who will be willing to die for all. On the night that Sirius dies, as Harry pursues Bellatrix Lestrange, Sirius's murderer, she mocks Harry and his godfather, speaking in a "mock-baby voice" and asking "did you *love* him, little baby Potter?" (*OP* 810). Thus as Harry's initiation continues and he must ponder still more incomprehensible certainties, he encounters those who cannot conceive of sacrificial love and those who mock parental love.

Another example of what Harry learns about this most profound mystery, human love, involves the character for whom he usually feels something very close to pure hatred: Professor Severus Snape. Whatever Potter readers may have expected to befall Snape or whatever new information about him they expected to come to light in the final book, it seems highly likely that Rowling surprised readers by the millions in *Deathly Hallows*. There readers discover that hateful Snape loved another—long ago, and always since. Moreover, Snape the Death Eater, the Dark Lord's spy, the killer of Dumbledore *is*, it turns out, loyal to Dumbledore and has lived the life of a double agent. Fewer than one-hundred pages from the end of 4100-page saga, readers fully understand and appreciate this rich literary character—the creation and development of whom, arguably, may be Rowling's crowning achievement. The murderous coward that eleven-year-old Harry hated for six years was, in truth, a devoted and brave man, probably the bravest Harry had ever known, as he will later tell his son named after Severus. In scene after scene in "The Prince's Tale" chapter of the final book, each more revealing than the last, scenes ranging from the recent past all the way back to Snape's sad boyhood, the picture finally becomes clear—not simplistically changing Snape from evil to good or from villain to hero. There is far more to the mysteries of Snape's life to warrant such simple transitions as those, and there was a sacred mystery that ordered his life.

Essentially in one chapter, Rowling changes Snape from caricature to character, from one whose actions seemed heartless but were actually heartfelt—and one who, unlike the Dark Lord whom Harry thought he served, could indeed love.

In Fitzgerald's *The Great Gatsby*, once Nick learns that Gatsby's house, parties, and ostentation are all because of his obsessive love for Daisy, Nick says of Gatsby: "He came alive to me, delivered suddenly from the womb of his purposeless splendor."[9] Once we know how Snape felt about Lily, once we hear him say the one word "Always," he is similarly delivered suddenly from the womb of his purposeless bitterness. As mysterious as many events and people are to Harry,

---

9   Nick's observation can be found in the Authorized Text of Fitzgerald's *The Great Gatsby* (New York: Collier, 1992) on page 83.

Snape has been no mystery at all: he is, to Harry, an unloving, unlovely, un-loyal, hateful man, incapable of love—one for whom Harry and most readers feel little pity or sympathy—until we learn his story and solve the mystery that *is* this man.

In "The Prince's Tale," when Snape shows Dumbledore that his Patronus is a silver doe (in memory of Harry's mother Lily), readers appreciate his life-long devotion to Lily, whom Snape had known long before she met and fell in love with Harry's father. Dumbledore asks Snape, "After all this time?" to which Snape simply answers, "Always" (*DH* 687). Very impressive is Rowling's decision not even to mention Lily's name here and not to comment further on Snape's love for her; nor does it seem a lack of restraint when the author ends the scene by having Dumbledore moved to tears when, of all people, Severus Snape, shows the effects in his life too of love, just love.

When Harry learns all this, sees all this in the Pensieve, he is literally floored as he lies "on the carpeted floor" of the headmaster's office (690). Moreover, it seems to Harry as if Snape has just, moments ago, left the office, has just closed the door. Ironically, a door has just now, finally, been opened for Harry—a great mystery that Harry did not even know *was* a mystery has been solved. Perhaps the greatest revelation of a mystery (lower case *m*) in the entire Potter series, Snape's true nature, is explained by perhaps the greatest Mystery (upper case *M*) beyond the pages of these or any books—love, or, again as Dumbledore would say, just love.

Before we leave the subject of love as a mystery, consider a passage in Proverbs (30: 18-19). Here the ancient writer confesses to being faced with some mysteries. How can these things be explained; who can understand them, he wonders: the way of an eagle in the air, the way of a serpent on a rock, the way of a ship in the midst of the sea, and the way of a man with a woman? In light of the two different kinds of mysteries with which Harry is faced and which we have been discussing, consider that long ago we have come to understand the aerodynamics of a bird's flight, the mobility of reptiles, and the principles of buoyancy. Yet, why *this* man loves *this* woman, or why *this* woman is willing to die for *this* man, or why *this* man and woman both know they wish to be together until eternity, remain mysteries—mysteries of a greater nature than Harry or Rowling or any one of us could ever solve—as incomprehensible as they are certain.

Many of Rowling's readers very early on assumed Dumbledore to be a god figure, much like Tolkien's Gandalf and Lewis's Aslan. In all of what the author calls the Wizarding world, Dumbledore seems uniquely omniscient, omnipotent, and, given his prowess in Apparition and invisibility, omnipresent. So, god-like, he seems to know the hearts of others; he certainly seems to know Harry's heart better than young Harry does himself. And it would seem that to read and know a human heart is to understand the profoundest of mysteries. Dumbledore, god-like, does just this on a number of occasions in the Potter books. In Book 6, he tells Harry that despite all the suffering and temptation Harry has endured, the boy remains "pure of heart, just as pure as you were at the age of eleven, when you stared into a mirror that reflected your heart's desire . . ." (511). Moreover, in *Order of the Phoenix*, just after Harry's godfather has been killed, Dumbledore tells him that feeling this pain is "part of being human"—to which Harry says he doesn't want to be human and screams, "I DON'T CARE!" (824). The headmaster, who knows Harry's true heart, then calmly says, "You care so much you feel as though you

will bleed to death with the pain of it." Later in Book
5, as he is reminding Harry of the "power" of love
Harry has in abundance, he explains that Voldemort
cannot bear to possess Harry, to penetrate his mind,
because, "[in] the end, it mattered not that you could
not close your mind. It was your heart that saved you"
(844). For those of us a bit less god-like than Albus
Dumbledore, however, these are indeed mysterious
explanations of mysteries.

Recall now that those who work behind the always-
locked door in the Department of Mysteries are known
as Unspeakables. The word *unspeakable* occurs three
times in the New Testament. St. Paul uses it twice
in his second letter to the Corinthians—referring
first to God's unspeakable gift and later to the man
caught up in paradise who hears unspeakable words
(2 Corinthians 9:15, 2 Corinthians 12:4). St. Peter says
that we rejoice with a joy unspeakable when we believe (1 Peter 1:8). Rowling's Unspeakables, a word that
clearly echoes the bible, are so named, we may assume,
because of the utmost secrecy of their work. These
Ministry of Magic employees are secretive within a secret place within a secret place. They are not allowed
to speak of their work and are thus aptly named. Yet,
even if they could speak, even if the door to the place
where the mystery of love is studied were unlocked,
even opened, what could the Unspeakables say?

What words could they speak to explain for example, with reference to Proverbs, the way of a man with
a woman? In his brilliant novel *Absalom, Absalom!*,
William Faulkner suggests that there are things for
which ten thousand words are too few and ten words
are too many, and that the story he is telling is one of
those things. So, it seems, is love one of those things;
for a great number of words or a very few well chosen ones might explain a mystery, but they will never
explain *mysterium*. And Harry, as we have seen, is

among the best at solving the former and among all the rest of us at trying during even the longest of lifetimes to understand the latter.

When Harry is taking Occlumency lessons with Professor Snape in *Order of the Phoenix*, he asks Snape, "What's in the Department of Mysteries?" (537). Snape's typically hostile and evasive answer is, "There are many things in the Department of Mysteries, Potter, few of which you would understand and none of which concern you . . ." (538). Professor Snape is only partially correct: though there are few of those mysteries, those incomprehensible certainties, that we would understand, *all* of them concern us and concern us profoundly. Rowling's mystery stories, read by hundreds of millions, may teach or remind us of nothing more than this: that they are not just about a boy and his friends solving interesting uncertainties; they are really about a young man and all of us older men and women who believe in the incomprehensible certainties of life, realizing that the only kinds of mysteries that ultimately matter *are* unsolvable—at least for the present. These *real* mysteries are what make us return to the Potter books again and again; they are what give depth to these otherwise formulaic, plot-driven books; they are what make Rowling's books a country for readers as young as Harry is in Book 1, as well as a country for old men and women and anyone in between.

I would like to close with a couple of personal anecdotes and a few literary analogies. Our youngest child, my daughter Alexi, was my last sidekick—that is, she rode shotgun with me, as her older siblings had done for many years before, on trips to the cleaners, the market, on deliveries to and pickups from school or soccer practice or music lessons. And speaking of music, we always had a cassette (Google that if you must) or a CD playing as we drove. One afternoon I slipped in Tchaikovsky's *Romeo and Juliet,* and as the music began, I told my daughter, who was about five or six years old at the time, the story of the star-crossed lovers, right down to the undelivered message and the lovers' demise. When Tchaikovsky's love theme near the end transitioned to the conflict theme, my daughter looked worried and suddenly said, "Wow, they're in trouble now."

And so they were—indeed *are*—whenever we read Shakespeare or listen to Tchaikovsky. But just as surely as the lovers will die, Romeo and Juliet will also live (they have for well over four hundred years). It is the music that keeps them going. Not long afterward, on another errand, my sidekick and I were listening to Pavarotti sing *Nessun Dorma.* I had not even attempted to explain the plot of *Turandot.* In fact, I think it is illegal in thirty-four states to drive and attempt to explain the plot of an opera at the same time. I just played the music with as non-intimidating an introduction as I could think of, saying something like, "Now, listen to *this.*" When the last note was sung and the triumphant *Vincerò!* was affirmed, my daughter asked, "Why does that sound so good even if I don't know what he's saying?"

To my daughter *Romeo and Juliet* were in trouble from the sound of the music alone, and Calaf sounded triumphant even though he sang in Italian. In both cases, the beautiful, communicative sounds came through and, later, the beautiful words that go with them can be learned and can augment the aesthetic experience—first the bangs and smoke, later the looking and the touching. First the interesting uncertainty, later the incomprehensible certainty.

So, again, why do we read and reread certain books and hear certain music that, as much as they reward us, leave us only wanting more? What is the answer to *that* mystery? How can it be explained? Edgar Allan Poe, in his magnificent essay "The Poetic Principle," contends that when we encounter something ineffably beautiful in poetry or music, when we are moved to tears by the power of it, we weep "not . . . through excess of pleasure, but through a certain, petulant, impatient sorrow at our inability to grasp *now*, wholly, here on earth, at once and for ever, those divine and rapturous joys, of which *through* the poem, or *through* the music, we attain to but brief and indeterminate glimpses."[10] Poe, who felt intensely that music is the ultimate source of beauty among mortals and whose aesthetics are essentially indistinguishable from his theology, affirms further: "We are often made to feel, with a shivering delight, that from an earthly harp are stricken notes which *cannot* have been unfamiliar to the angels."

I know I've drifted pretty far out to sea here, and I've probably painted myself into a corner (not to mention having mixed metaphors) in suggesting, through Poe, that music may explain the mystery of extraordinary reader rewards like those that millions get from Rowling. Music explaining a mystery of a magical reading experience is reminiscent of Churchill's line about Russia: "a riddle, wrapped in a mystery, inside an enigma." Yet, maybe this musical matter is not as crazy as it first sounds, and maybe I am not painted in that corner alone. After all, Dumbledore, moved to tears by the students' singing, proclaims, "Ah music . . . A magic beyond all we do here" (*SS* 128). Poe might agree if I tweaked the homonym and suggested that

---

10   Excerpts from *"The Poetic Principle"* can be found in *The Portable Edgar Allan Poe, edited by J. Gerald Kennedy (New York: Penguin, 2006). These quotations are on page 561.*

the magic in the music is both *beyond all we do here* and *beyond all we do hear.*

I have tried to explain how great works take us from mystery to Mystery, from bangs-magic to touching-magic, and from mortal music to that of the angels. You would think that is a long journey and a hard trip, but when we ride as shotgun-sidekicks with the ones who have driven us so well, we hardly know how fast, far, and fabulously they are moving us. Rowling, I firmly believe, like so many other musicians, can take us from here to there, from an interesting uncertainty to an incomprehensible certainty, just as naturally and pleasantly as I used to take my daughter to her music lessons and back home again.

CHAPTER 7 --- JOHN GRANGER

Alliteration and Echoing in Harry Potter Names

Reading At A Level Beyond Tit-for-Tat Allegory

YOU WOULD HAVE TO be fairly inattentive not to be struck by Ms. Rowling's fondness for alliteration in her Harry Potter novels. She uses the repeated first sound of a word in naming persons (Peter Pettigrew), places (Ministry of Magic), things (Smelting Stick), animals (Buckbeak/Witherwing), plants (Whomping Willow), events (the TriWizard Tournament), even school subjects (Defense Against the Dark Arts, a **D**oubly **A**lliterative D-a-D-a).

It's hardly surprising, then, that the Weasley twins, alliteration incarnate as mirror images, have a special fondness for initial repetition, if Weasley's Wizard Weezes is still a delight and the contents of a Skiving Snackbox are exactly what you'd expect from playful, literate twins: Puking Pastilles, Fever Fudge, Canary Creams, Ton Tongue Toffee, and Nosebleed Nougat.

In a recent Potter Pundit talk, we three went on at some length about name meanings without discussing why Ms. Rowling might care for comic alliteration and otherwise risible names. What I want to explore today is (1) both alliteration and the remarkable internal echoing in *Harry Potter* character names, (2) from which authors Ms. Rowling might have picked up this fascinating signature, and (3), most importantly, how this alliteration and internal echoing reflects and reinforces the most profound meanings of the seven Hogwarts Saga novels.

We'll start with some lists of names for a warm-up. Or should I say "laughable lists of nonsensical names for a wild and woolly warm-up"? Take your pick.

Alliteration, Repeated Letters, and Internal Resonances in Potter Names

The 'Four Founders' are an obviously alliterative group for our beginning: Godric Gryffindor, Salazar Slytherin, Rowena Ravenclaw, and Helga Huffelpuff. And the Heads of Houses? Not too surprisingly, as they represent the Four Founders in some respect, we have Minerva McGonagall, Severus Snape, Filius Flitwick, and Pomona Sprout. They are joined on the faculty, at least for a short while, by **Quirr**ius **Quirr**ell and **M**ad-Eye **M**oody.

And the Ghosts and Ghouls on campus? The Fat Friar, the Bloody Baron, Nearly-headless Nick, Moaning Myrtle, and Peeves the Poltergeist. The Grey Lady is important, too, but I'll have to come back to her.

Really, surveying any list of Harry Potter character names, it's hard to miss the up-front repetition in the labels Ms. Rowling gives the inhabitants of her subcreation. Say these names aloud to catch the effect:

Archibald Alderton, Arkie Alderton, Bathsheba Babbling, Bathilda Bagshot, Blodwyn Bludd, Barberus Bragge, Betty Braithwaite, Broderick Bode, Cho Chang, Colin Creevey, Dilys Derwent, Daedulus Diggle, (Elphias) "Dog breath" Doge, Dudley Dursley, Gellert Grindelwald, Filius Flitwick, Florean Fortescue, Gladys Gudgeon, Gregory Goyle, Luna Lovegood, Madames Malkin and March, Pansy Parkinson, Patma and Parvati Patil, Piers Polkiss, Stan Shunpike, Thaddeus Thurkell, Ted Tonks, Tilden Toots, William Weasley, Willy Widdershins, and Vindinctus Viridian.

That preponderant alliteration is simultaneously fun and fascinating but the repetition of sounds in Ms. Rowling's character names isn't limited to the initial consonants. Non-alliterative names, i.e., those not beginning with the same letter, often include reduplicated sounds, paired letters, or both.

As an example of reduplicated sounds, note the 'c's (and 'k') as well as the 'a's and 'r's in 'Caratacus Burke.' How about the 'n's and 'o's in 'Antonin Dolohov'? The Hogwarts Headmaster's name rolls off the tongue as pleasantly, even melodiously, as it does because of the repetition in alternation of the 'b's and 'd's in it: 'Albus Dumbledore.' This pairing and resonance is obviously a little less obvious (!) than alliteration, but the internal echoing of sounds in Ms. Rowling's name choices has a similar, musical effect.

Roll these several names off your tongue and note the echoes inside them of repeated vowels and consonants: Justin Finch-Fletchley, Alecto Carrow, Fleur Delacour, Vernon Dursley, Angelina Johnson, Viktor Krum, and, yes, the Grey Lady.

Along with these echoes, Ms. Rowling loves paired letters which have much the same effect as re-duplicated sounds except the pairing makes the sound 'jump' because of the proximity of the echo to its source. Hannah Abbot, Neville Longbottom, and, most importantly, Harry Potter are instances of this.

These three names with paired letters are unusual, though, in that they don't also feature either internal echoes or up-front alliteration. Pairings usually come with one or the other of these naming echoes. Enjoy noting both the letter pairings and the internal echoes of these Hogwarts Saga names: Cuthbert Binns, Reginald Cattermole, Dirk Cresswell, Cedric Diggory, Arabella Doreen Figg, and Seamus Finnegan. Perhaps my favorite name in the series is Peter Pettigrew, whose name, in addition to being especially revealing about his character (and funny), simultaneously features alliterative initial consonants, a sound pairing, and internal echoes of 'p's, 't's, 'e's, *and* 'r's.

This represents quite the pattern. Is there any reason, to think Ms. Rowling puts this kind of care into her name choices?

Ms. Rowling, if Accio Quotes is to be believed (always!), "collects names; some characters had 8 or 9 names before she found the right one. **Naming is 'crucial' to her.**"[11] Most of the attention serious readers give these names, though, is on the surface meanings of the names: what the name means literally or the person to whom it refers. "Crookshanks" is an excellent example.

Anyone with a decent SAT verbal score and a moment to reflect recognizes the joke in Hermione's pet's name. It is a comic pointer to his being bandy-legged (crooked-shanks). The better joke, though, and the reason the cat/kneazle is bandy-legged is in Ms. Rowling's

---

11   http://www.accio-quote.org/themes/names.htm

tip of the hat to George Cruikshank, famous English caricaturist and Dickens illustrator. Crookshanks, whose intelligence and insight Sirius admires as much as Lupin admires Hermione's brains (pets always resemble their owners, right?), has the piercing ability to see beyond the surface of things, hence his recognition that a certain oversized black dog and rat missing a finger weren't just what they seemed. 'Crookshanks' with bowed legs as a pointer to George Cruikshank, brilliant satirist, gives us an insight to the animal character so named and a chuckle, too.

I'm guessing if you're a regular at HogwartsProfessor. com that you're accustomed to analysis of names in Harry Potter that follow this Crookshanks pattern: break down the words in their name to dope out their several meanings along with a search for any relevant referents that might be in it as well. When we play the Dickensian Cryptonym game there, those are the rules of engagement for the most part. What I am wondering, after playing this game for more than a few years now, if in toying with the surface meanings of Ms. Rowling's remarkable name-play, we haven't neglected the surface of these names, quite literally the letters that make them up, and missed a much greater meaning hidden in them.

Could it be, to keep to our example, that for understanding 'Crookshanks" it is almost as important for us to note that we have paired 'o's and echoed 'k's in the name of Hermione's cat/kneazle? I think it might.

Likely Literary Antecedents: Nabokov, Hugo, and Dickens

Having established that Ms. Rowling enjoys names of a certain construction — alliterative, with paired

letters, and having internal resonances or echoes —
before I get to *why* she chooses to do this and *what* it
may mean, I want to make a short diversion to note
that she isn't the first author to do this. I think the
sort of names she prefers to give her characters are
reminiscent of at least three authors that she cares for:
Nabokov, Hugo, and Dickens.

Ms. Rowling has said more than once that her three
favorite writers are Jane Austen, Colette, and Vladimir
Nabokov.[12] This last author is usually a surprise to her
fans because, consequent to prurient readings of his
Lolita, Nabokov is often dismissed as "pornographic,"
which description, whatever one makes of the several
snogging moments in *Harry Potter*, I have not found
in even the most deranged Harry Hater's critiques
of the series. Nabokov's novels, however, are famous
among the more literate for their "complex plots, clever word play, and [their] use of alliteration."[13] You don't
need even to read *Lolita* to see the sort of resonance
we've been talking about in the title character Lolita's
name and the Potter-esque echoes in the names of the
book's principal male characters, Humbert Humbert
and Claire Quilty. [Nabokov shared the name of his
father so he was known as "Vladimir Vladimirovich"
and included a character in *Lolita* whose name was an
anagram of his own (**Vivi**an Dark**bloo**m). Echoes and
word play, you might say, came naturally to him.]

I wrote a short post at HogwartsProfessor[14] about the
influence of Victor Hugo on Harry Potter and the hat-
tip to the alchemical French novelist's *Les Miserable*s

---

12   *E.g.,* **Q:** *Who are your favorite writers now?* **Rowling:** *Jane
Austen, Nabokov, Colette.*

http://www.angelfire.com/mi3/cookarama/sydherint00.html
13   *http://en.wikipedia.org/wiki/Vladimir_Nabokov*
14   *http://www.hogwartsprofessor.com/harry-potter-and-victor-hugos-
cosette/*

Ms. Rowling makes in Harry's living under the stairs and in the character named Hugo, the son of Ron and Hermione Weasley. That novel's female leads, Cosette and her mother Fantine, have names with letter pairings and internal resonances, but it is in the story's hero, **Jean** Valjean, that we see the real mirroring. As if to make the point about the importance of this "Jean" echoing, Hugo tells us that Jean's father's name was Jean Valjean, his mother's name was Jeanne Valjean, and the sister who raised him after their deaths, you guessed it, was also Jeanne Valjean.

As interesting and as suggestive as the Nabokov and Hugo influences on Ms. Rowling's naming signatures may be, they pale before the master of literary names, Charles Dickens, whose character cryptonyms in addition to having layered meanings, also feature alliteration, letter pairings, and internal echoes. I've discussed the influence of Dickens on Rowling as an alchemical writer at HogwartsProfessor[15] and it is a pretty big part of *Harry Potter's Bookshelf* (see the Orphan-*bildungsroman* chapter as well as the literary alchemy piece), but the most obvious link between Ms. Rowling and arguably the greatest or at least "more revered" English novelist is in the names.

To get to character names, let's start with alliteration and a few of Dickens' better known book titles, a title being the name of the novel: *Tale of Two Cities, Christmas Carol, Pickwick Papers,* and *Nicholas Nickleby.* Those are surely familiar. Warmed up? Okay, here are my favorite character names from Dickens' novels, in sequence, preceded by the name of the book in italics, all of which have been chosen because of their alliterative initials, paired letters, and internal resonances.

Pickwick Papers: Augustus Snodgrass, Arabella Allen, Samuel Weller; *Nicholas Nickleby:* Newman Noggs; *Barnaby Rudge; Martin Chuzzlewit:* Seth Pecksniff, Montague Tigg (aka Tigg Montague!), Mrs. Lupin (not alliterative or resonant, I know, but I couldn't leave out Mark Tapley's innkeeper friend and distant relation, no doubt, of Remus Lupin!), *David Copperfield:* aka David *Trottwood* Copperfield, Clara Copperfield, Edward Murdstone, 'umble Uriah Heep, Clara Peggotty, Tommy Traddles, Wilkins Micawber; *Bleak House:* Esther Summerson, Allan Woodcourt, John Jarndyce, Jarndyce & Jarndyce (the family curse), Bayham Badger, Caddy Jellyby; *Hard Times:* Thomas Gradgrind; *Little Dorrit;* Flora Flinching; *Our Mutual Friend:* Rogue Riderhood; *Edwin Drood:* John Jasper, Canon Chrisparkle, and Dick Datchery.

The two Dickens stories you can assume most folks have read are *Christmas Carol* and *Tale of Two Cities.* In *Carol*, we meet 'Tiny Tim' Cratchitt, kindly Mr Fezzlewigg, and, of course, Ebenezer Scrooge. *Tale of Two Cities* features Charles Darnay, Sydney Carton, Jarvice Lorry, Alexander Manette, and the dominatrix Madame Defarge.

If Harry Potter's name is a direct Dickens descendant, though, he most surely has his blood-lines from the protagonist of *Great Expectations*, Philip Pirrip, also known as 'Pip.' Resonances, alliteration, repeated letters, and two near palindromes!

So What? The Meaning of Repetition, Reflection, and Resonance in Potter Names

Okay, so Ms. Rowling isn't the first to have done this. So what? Why do I care as a serious reader that writers like Charles Dickens, Victor Hugo, Vladimir Nabokov, and Joanne Rowling seem to be very careful in choosing names to give us alliteration, internal echoes from first name to family name or within either one, and with paired letters?

First, a note to the skeptics: yes, I understand that not every character and not even *most* characters in either Dickens' (with his 989 named characters...) or Rowling's work has a name that fits this pattern. And, yes, I do know that too much can be made of this. Having a restricted number of sounds and letters, names made up of these letters will necessarily involve some repetition.

Taking two groups at random, my brothers — **Lawren**ce (**Larry**) **A**nthony **Granger**, Stephen (Steve) **W**ayne **Granger**, **A**lan Scott **Granger**– and the Potter Pundits– Jame**s** **T**homas, **T**ravis **Prinzi**, John **Granger**, we see in their names all of the things I'm saying great writers do — and none of our parents, that I know of, were especially literary or inclined to either cryptonyms or word-play. My father once said that 'Anthony' was the name of a janitor he admired at the business where he was a plant manager and that 'Alan Scott' came from a comic book he read in a barbershop (if true, he must have picked up a 'Golden Age' Green Lantern adventure) but that's all we got for 'meaning.' This can be overdone.

Having acknowledged that, I think we can still claim these patterns are significant and worthy of our attention as Potter-philes for three reasons.

(1) It seems to be a signature of writers who are not only considered 'Greats' but who also have a hermetic or symbolist intention in writing. Dickens, Rowling, and Hugo all wrote novels that have alchemical scaffolding or symbols in them to highlight and re-inforce their meanings of human transformation and redemption.

(2) Ms. Rowling has marked not every or, again, even *most* of her characters with names of this type but she has labeled the Four Founders, the Heads of Houses, the Ghosts, the Headmaster, a gaggle of major characters from Neville Longbottom and Peter Pettigrew, and the title protagonist of the series, the hero, with such names.

(3) The nature of *names* themselves as a type of word invites reflection on meaning.

This last invites some explanation, too. Hang on here; deep water ahead.

All words per se, as signifiers of a specific referent, are names. Usually, though, and in this discussion, too, we are using the word 'names' as a signifier for a subset *within* the larger category 'words' for those words that are used to denote and describe specific people, here fictional characters. We use names as symbols or signs, in effect; if I say the words 'John Granger,' 'Harry Potter,' or 'Daedalus Diggle,' the words bring up associated memories and experiences.

Real world names for people act as symbols in that our surnames, a rule with many exceptions, reflect a "patronymic, profession, or place,' i.e., most family names tell other people who our father or what our clan is, what we do for a living, or where we are from. Personal (first names) or nicknames have sometimes subtle, sometimes obvious meanings to everyone that hears or sees them; you know this because you have met people like I have whose given names were 'Stacey Ferguson' which they changed to 'Anastasia Monique Applebury' to reflect they no longer wanted to be just "another girl from Arkansas." No joke.

And names are powerful symbols, too. They act, for example, in the case of Divine Names, as transparencies and translucencies, even points of communion with the Absolute. All the great revealed traditions revere a Name, the invocation of Which will bring the believer into the Presence of the Named (read Metropolitan Kallistos Ware's *The Power of the Name* or *Way of a Pilgrim* for the traditional Christian way to sanctification via invocation, the way that is the heart, some say, of Eastern Christian monasticism).

Names of characters in literature are different than names of people in the street because (a) authors have more freedom than parents do in naming their progeny, not to mention the omniscience to know how their child will 'turn out,' and (b) better authors are intentionally using character names as pointers to the symbolic freight, role, or destiny their character is carrying in the story s/he is writing. Names of characters, then, are best understood as symbols, or better, transparencies, through which the writer is telling us to look in order to understand the character named, a character that is a transparency, too.

A well-conceived name, then, is a **symbol *of the story symbol*** so named, and, like its character-referent, it should be a window through we can see whatever allegorical meaning the author is inspired to share with her or his readers.

It won't surprise those who have read my books that I think the best stories and symbols are understood most clearly when interpreted at four levels (why this is the case — the correspondence of the four ways of human knowing with reality — is explained at HogwartsProfessor.com and in *Spotlight,* my book on the *Twilight* saga[16]). Ms. Rowling herself points to

---

16   See *http://www.hogwartsprofessor.com/on-critical-reception-of-*

this traditional approach within *Deathly Hallows* by including a symbol — the triangulated and bisected circle representing the three Hallows — inside her narrative that the characters interpret in the traditional four meanings: surface, moral, allegorical, and anagogical (it's all in *Deathly Hallows Lectures,* so I won't spell that out here). I think, if we keep in mind that names are symbol-symbols or tokens for the story symbols the named characters are, that we should interpret names on the same four levels.

The **surface** meaning of names includes the simple stuff like what clan the person named belongs to. The reaction people have when they meet Draco or Ron for the first time tells us that names work as surname or family signifiers in the magical worlds the same way they do in 'real life.' Meeting a Malfoy or Weasley boy means something to people because they make the surface associations with other Malfoys or Weasleys they have met or heard about.

The next aspect of surface reading is just noting what the names mean as words, especially if there are homophones involved. 'Crookshanks' sounds like 'crooked shanks' which means bow-legged and the cat is bow-legged. Pretty straight forward. Sirius Black sounds like "serious black,' which suggests darkness, even danger, which, when we hear about him in *Prisoner of Azkaban*, is exactly what he represents.

This bleeds rather neatly into the moral or social layer of meaning. Translate 'Draco Malfoy" into English and you get 'Serpent BadFaith.' I don't care how you cut that, you're meant to lump this guy, along with 'Narcissist BadFaith' and 'LightBearing (Lucifer) BadFaith' his parents, into the scary bin. 'Godric Gryffindor,' in contrast, parses to 'Godly

harry-potter-and-twilight-part-5-iconological-criticism-and-best-sellers-a/ and http://spotlightontwilight.com/spotlight_intro.pdf

GoldenGriffin.' That bears a little more interpretation than 'Serpent BadFaith,' but the 'Godly' cues us in to his probably being on the side of the angels, literally or figuratively speaking.

Miriam Greenwald wrote at Hogwarts Professor[17] that names can have a social meaning at their surface in being ludicrous. She argues, I think convincingly, that in a more formal culture there is satirical weight in naming characters with the ludicrously heavy 'Justin Finch-Fletchley' and 'Wilhemina Grubbly-Plank' and 'Sir Patrick Delaney-Podmore.'

Most of the fun, though, in interpreting names — and almost all of the work to date — has been on the allegorical level, as we saw with Crookshanks-George Cruikshank above. The first step here is to catch the real-world referent. James Thomas noted on the Potter Pundits show on names, for example, that Cornelius Oswald Fudge's middle name is poison on both sides of the Atlantic; Americans think of JFK's assassin, Lee Harvey Oswald, and Brits are reminded of the founder of the British Union of Fascists, Oswald Mosley. 'Remus Lupin' is both a real-world (mythological!) reference and a description; Remus was one of the twin founders of Rome, both of which boys were suckled by a wolf, and 'Lupin' is doggone close to 'lupine,' meaning 'wolf-like.'

It's tempting to wade into this field and start listing all the names and their corresponding historical, mythical, and other-worldly referents, but you can find such lists on the Internet and in more pedestrian guidebooks to the series. They are books worth buying and sites worth visiting (try Veritaserum, MuggleNet, and the Harry Potter Lexicon, for starters), certainly

---

17   *http://www.hogwartsprofessor.com/dickensian-names-and-victorian-sensibilities/*

because each name's referents (and often there are several, a point we'll have to come back to) open up the symbolism of the character in the story.

With a player who only appears once on stage, it can serve as a critical clue for understanding his or her meaning. Charity Burbage, for example, has a first name meaning 'Love' and a last name pointing us to Richard Burbage, the original Shakespearean actor. Her placement — and grisly execution — at the beginning of *Deathly Hallows* clues us to be ready for Love's victory over death at story's end and the apotheosis of the hero in the drama, a Shakespearean signature.

I have to confess, though, that I have found the lists I have read that "define" a name's meaning less than satisfying. They are, as a rule, simultaneously enriching and frustrating, even annoying. On the one hand, I always learn something on these sites. Who knew, for instance, that Mulciber was "a character in John Milton's *Paradise Lost*, … a fallen angel who is the architect of Pandemonium, the capital of Hell and home to the demons' council"[18]? I didn't. Did you know that 'Alastor' is Scottish for 'Alexander'? that 'Cho' is Korean for 'beautiful'?[19] Me, neither. I love prowling these list sites.

On the other hand, these lists usually leave me shaking my head. The information inevitably fails on one or more of three counts. They are wrong, they are closed doors, or (often it's *and*) they neglect the obvious and the sublime. They almost never take the time to explain how even the one meaning given illumines the meaning of the character so named.

---

18   http://www.angelfire.com/mi3/cookarama/namemean.html

19   *http://www.veritaserum.com/info/misc/babynames.shtml*

Take the entry for 'Colin' at Mugglenet's Name page: **Colin** – *Means "youth, child, or victor." Also means "young dog," which fits his devotion to Harry.*[20] Or try Veritaserum.com's Name Meaning List: *Colin (Greek) – A short form of Nicholas (Nicholas means young cub).*[21]

I studied Greek in High School and College, and, though I was no great shakes as a Classics Major, I know that's not right. So I went to a baby names web site and looked up 'Colin." Here is what they have:

The boy's name **Colin** \c(o)-lin\ is pronounced *KOH-lin, KAH-lin*. It is of Irish, Scottish and Gaelic origin, and its meaning is "young creature". Diminutive form of the medieval name Col or Colle, a short form of **Nicholas** (Greek) "people of victory."[22]

I'd want to argue with that, too; I've been told by Orthodox Christians who actually speak Greek that it means "victory of the people" and is a name of Christ, like most Saints' names from the first centuries *anno Domini*. But with either "people of victory" or "victory of the people," we're a long way from "young cub," right? It works for 'Col' but not for Nicholas.

But those kind of errors are what you expect from internet resources.

What makes me shudder is the confidence with which the answer is given at Mugglenet and Veritaserum and how quickly the door is closed on further discussion of Colin Creevey's name. I imagine the name-seeker saying to him or herself: "'Colin' means "young cub,'

20   *http://www.mugglenet.com/books/name_origins_characters.shtml*
21   *Op.cit; veritaserum.com*
22   *http://www.thinkbabynames.com/meaning/1/Colin*

Colin Creevey is a younger student and kind of an annoying pet to Harry and friends, got it." The one-liner is wrong and the equation with the character the definition assumes the reader will make is vacant.

But, really, we're a long way from the meaning of Colin Creevey. And this isn't just a Veritaserum.com problem. Check out these sites:

> **Creevey: Colin** is derived from Nicholas, "victorious people." **Dennis** means "wild" or "frenzied." Creevey is an actual English surname, but no meaning has yet been uncovered.[23] (angelfire. com, see note 18)
> *"Creeve" ="to burst," suggesting the Creevey brothers' excitability.*[24]
> **Creevey** – A common surname. From Irish origin, meaning 'prolific' – possibly a reference to the creevey brothers' persistence or from *"Creeve" ="to burst," suggesting the Creevey brothers' excitability.*[25]

Overlooking what seems to be the outright theft from the Lexicon in the Mugglenet definition, we're stuck at the surface level of these symbols, even if we *can* find a decent definition for the words involved. If we cannot go any further, we should still try, as the Lexicon does with "creeve" above, to make a connection with the characters involved. The definition isn't an explanation or understanding in itself.

I want to note here, that even with the sites that give decent definitions and try to make the allegorical connections like 'Mulciber' above, 'Argus Filch,' and 'Mundungus Fletcher' with literary, mythic, and

---

23   *Op.cit., angelfire.com*
24   *http://www.hplex.info/wizards/a-z/c.html*
25   *Op.cit., MuggleNet.com*

earthy meanings ('mundungus,' we're told, is a type of noxious tobacco), the connection between definition or referent and the character involved is, more often than not, left to the reader and left at one level.

I stumbled on the 'Colin' example because it was right beneath 'Cho,' a name I picked randomly as I looked for one I didn't know for this list. But it caught my eye, not only because I knew the Nicholas definition was funky, but also because 'Colin Creevey' is a pointer to two specific characters, Colin Craven of *The Secret Garden* and Sara Crewe of *A Little Princess*, created by an author Ms. Rowling has obviously read closely and admired, Frances Hodgson-Burnett.

Because you've read *Harry Potter's Bookshelf* (and, yes, if you haven't, you really must), you know the depth of Ms. Rowling's debt to Hodgson-Burnett. I don't want to use the space here to detail the specifics and themes Ms. Rowling lifted in large part from this author — you can read them in the opening paragraphs of 'Secret Doctrine of *The Secret Garden*' at HogwartsProfessor.com[26] — but it should suffice to say that the esoteric Christian meaning of eyes in Harry Potter owes quite a bit to the eyes of a 'Mother' and of a dead mother named Lillias in *Garden*.

If you believe that this is an isolated instance, an exceptional exception if you will to the usually credible way of thinking about the meaning of names in one-line definitions as translations, you're not giving Ms. Rowling sufficient credit as a name cryptographer. She is, quite frankly, as careful in crafting her names, the symbols representing her archetypal characters, as she is in the characters themselves.

---

26   *http://www.hogwartsprofessor.com/the-secret-doctrine-of-the-secret-garden/*

We've already discussed the several meanings of Crookshanks, whom, I trust, most readers will agree is not a central character in the novels. My *How Harry Cast His Spell* devotes a chapter to the more interesting names of the principals in the series, more recently Travis Prinzi has posted on the meaning of Albus Dumbledore's involved name at TheHogsHead.org, and the Potter Pundits have done an entire hour just skimming the subject (soon to be re-broadcast as a PotterCast stand-alone show). But just to give another example of what a one-liner definition/translation can miss, take 'Sirius Black.'

I mentioned above when talking about reading a name's surface meaning that 'Sirius Black' can and should be read as 'serious black.' The character, when we first hear about him from Muggle television and then from Cornelius Fudge in the Three Broomsticks, is a seriously black figure, something like the heart of darkness. He is the man who betrayed Harry's parents, murdered Peter Pettigrew, and escaped Azkaban to hunt Harry as a service to the Dark Lord. Doesn't get much more seriously black than that.

But we learn that the surface meaning, beyond denoting the melancholy of a man having spent more than a decade with the Dementors and whose best friends were murdered consequent to his mistake in judgment, is not the real or only meaning. 'Sirius' is the name of the brightest star in the night sky and is also known as 'the Dog Star.' Sirius Black, then, means 'Black Dog,' which, of course, turns out to be the form Harry's godfather assumes when he becomes an Animagus. This is the definition-translation you will find on the one-liner name-meaning web sites.

The problem is that this tit-for-tat point-to-point name-to-referent translation misses the heart of what

Sirius' name is about. Serious readers of Harry Potter are familiar with the alchemical scaffolding and symbolism on which Ms. Rowling has built the Hogwarts Saga and how *Order of the Phoenix*, the fifth book which features Sirius and The House of Black, is the series *nigredo* or 'black' stage. Not noting this aspect of 'black' means missing out on why Sirius dies at the end of *Phoenix*, marking the end of the black stage just as characters named 'white' and 'red' die at the end of *Half-Blood Prince* and *Deathly Hallows*. That's not a small thing.

And alchemy and astrology are paired traditional sciences and symbolisms. Most of Sirius' relations are named for stars and two different Potter scholars have contributed essays to the second volume of *The Hog's Head Conversations* that explore the relevance of these names. I have to think that Sirius' first name will prove to be as meaning-laden as his surname.

I dwell on this at such length for two reasons.

First, I think the one-liner translation fails as definition because it rarely notes multiple meanings and shadings, and, more important, as a rule to which I have found no exception, it never gets beyond the allegorical, tit-means-tat level. There is no acknowledgment of a fourth level of symbolic meaning, the anagogical or sublime, not to mention no attempt to explore it. Albus Dumbledore is a 'white bumble-bee,' Sirius Black is a 'black dog,' Crookshanks is 'bow-legged,' and Colin Creevey is an 'excitable victor-pup.'

Why do Potter etymologists and serious readers trusting their definitions find these superficial explanations satisfying? In a word, 'nominalism,' the spirit of our Age and the last three or four Ages, truth be told. We live in a world of superficial understandings in which quantities of matter and energy in their various stages of transformation, solid to plasma, are understood as the only empirical, objective reality. The advocates of a qualitative understanding of the world, the counterweight to nominalists like William of Ockham, were the philosophical realists, who thought that truth, beauty, and goodness were the inside far greater than the outside of measurable surface quantities. This kind of realist, we'd call them idealists or Romantics, last held sway in the Public Square when the Cambridge Platonists made a heroic rear guard action back in the 17th century. Artists, preachers, and dreamers now are second-class citizens in a world of mathematicians and scientists.

Ms. Rowling points to her preference for the Platonists of old and her disdain for nominalists and empiricists of today in her creating a magical world devoid of technology in which the people without imagination and magic are Muggles. As I explained in a HogwartsProfessor.com post about Muggletonians, John Everard, William Penn, Seekers, and the historical time witches and wizards disappeared,[27] Ms. Rowling's world-view is revolutionary and traditional. [I'll be talking about this at Infinitus in Orlando.]

One of my favorite pointers to this is that they don't teach "Math" at Hogwarts, but "Arithmancy,' sometimes called numerology, which, if memory serves, Hermione says is her favorite subject. Arithmancy differs from arithmetic that Muggles study in being a qualitative study of number and geometry rather than a quantitative one. The number 'one,' for instance, understood this way is a symbol of unity, unification, integrity, eternity, and the whole; a little different than thinking of it as a signifier for a solitary 'unit,' no?

27   *http://www.hogwartsprofessor.com/john-everard-the-original-seeker/*

[This is important for understanding *Harry Potter*, as I explain in *Harry Potter Unlocked*, because of the symbolist meaning of the number seven which pervades the series, from the number of books and years at Hogwarts to the number of Quidditch players and Horcruxes. Note, too, that conventional as opposed to Pythagorean numerology turns largely on the interpretation of names.]

Traditional people differ from moderns largely in how they understand and experience number and space (geometry). To the philosophical realists, mathematics and geometry were almost a mystery religion, to risk hyperbole, and certainly an introduction to metaphysics and seeing the world sacramentally, that is, looking at things as transparencies through which invisible, greater truths could be known. Luna Lovegood, the spiritual and cosmological aspects of whose name was discussed at length in a Potter Pegment segment devoted to her (*Harry Potter Smart Talk*, chapter 1), sees things just this way, hence her ability to answer the Ravenclaw door's question with an answer about the meaning of a circle, an answer which allowed her and Harry into the inside bigger than the outside not visible at the surface.

The Ravenclaw door thought Luna's answer was "well reasoned" but I'm sure if she had offered this kind of answer to a Muggle math teacher that she would have been sent in to have her medication adjusted. What's odd to me — and to bring this back to names — is that Muggle math teachers and students think they understand number because they have facility getting answers to problems. My experience has been that this reflects the shallowest of understandings, not only in its denial of a greater qualitative meaning, but even in the meaning of quantitative number and mathematical operations.

If you doubt this, ask a math teacher or high school student to explain the division of fractions. Unless they are Luna-types, they will inevitably tell you how to solve a division of fractions problem, which is to say, the mechanics of getting an answer. If you interrupt to ask what they are doing, as in, how the process could be used (as they surely could do if asked to explain subtracting integers or adding fractions), they look at you dumbfounded. Dividing fractions is about getting the right answer, period. Remember Umbridge's comment about "this isn't the real world, Ms. Granger, it is *school*"? This isn't thinking about number, it's *school*.

The way we approach names in Harry Potter, unfortunately, reflects the nominalist blindness we have from our education and culture. We want the *answer*, the one-line connection between the item in column a and the corresponding correct value in column b. The definitions or translations to be found in Harry Potter guides and websites are about names understood as signs rather than symbols.

A stop sign, the red thing we find posted on street corners, means one thing and it is undeniably a social fact rather than a transparency to an eternal verity (I have no trouble imagining a world in which stop signs are yellow and square rather than the red shape I was trained to recognize and I'm sure there is a history of the evolution of stop signs somewhere on the internet). Signs are good and useful things — and it's wonderful that they don't have multiple meanings (if it is curious that American drivers always think the red sign means "SLOW").

Symbols, though, differ from signs in having multiple possible meanings or levels of meaning and in being passageways to greater understanding or even to realities greater than themselves. Interpreting a

symbol as a sign or marker for one meaning is to have
missed almost entirely the substance or end of the
symbol.

Which brings me at last to the three fascinating
patterns we found earlier, patterns that are prevalent
in the names of Dickens characters and the popula-
tion of Ms. Rowling's *Harry Potter* novels: **alliteration** or repetition of the initial letter, **internal echoing** or repetition of a sound in the first and surnames
or within either one, and **paired letter**s. You cannot
get anything more superficial than these patterns because they are patterns in the letters representing the
sounds of the names rather than their referent meanings. I think, though, that these patterns all point to
two of Ms. Rowling's major themes in her work, both
of which are anagogical or sublime, which is to say
"anything but superficial."

Doppelgangers, Mirrors, and What It Means to be Human

When you're talking about repetition and echoes
with respect to character symbols, the word that
should pop into our collective consciousness is 'dop-
pelgangers.' This staple of 19th century Gothic and romantic fiction is a creature or pair of creatures that
have complementary figures or shadows, which shadows reveal aspects of their otherwise invisible character. Think of Stevenson's *Jekyll & Hyde*, Shelley's *Dr.
Frankenstein* and his monster, and the *Count of Monte
Cristo*. Rowling points to these shadows in her principal characters in a variety of ways:

<u>*As Animagi:*</u> How many animagi do we know of in
the books? James, Sirius, Peter, Minerva, and Rita, for
starters, and I'll add Albus who certainly as a former
Master of Transfiguration at Hogwarts and alchemist
has mastered this trick (I still think he must be the

tawny owl that appears in several places). Nymphadora
Tonks as a shape changer (Metamorphmagus) deserves a special mention.

Half-breeds/mudbloods/monsters: Half-breeds and
mudbloods as well as two natured monsters include
Hagrid, Olympe, Fleur, Lily, Tom Riddle, Hermione,
Remus, Tonks again and Severus (allowing that he is
some sort of vampire!). Harry, because he grew up as a
Muggle, has an honorary membership here.

Threshhold characters (the 'Liminal'): these are the
folks in Potterworld that live in two worlds or so far
to the periphery of their own worlds that they cannot
fit into the usual categories (good guy or Death Eater,
for instance). Snape leads this group, Dobby is a close
second, Firenze, Hagrid, Remus, Peter, Neville, squibs
Argus and Arabella, Mundungus, and Percy – despite
his Battle of Hogwarts redemption – fill out the set.

Twins, Pairs, and Brothers: George and Fred, the
Weasley troop, Hagrid and Grawp, the Creevey brothers, Sirius and James, Crabbe and Goyle, Ron and
Hermione, Slytherin and Gryffindor, Lily and Petunia,
Lily and Narcissa (flowers of the same family), Peter
and Neville (a cross-generational pair of look-alikes),
Harry and Dudley, and Harry and Neville (joined by
the prophecy). And those Patils!
Harry/Voldemort: *Order of the Phoenix* begins with
three mentions of Harry's feeling that his skull has
been split in two and one has to imagine it must crack
right down that jagged scar. It turns out that Harry's
head really is divided and he has an unwelcome guest.
He isn't carrying a passenger like Quirrell or possessed
as was Ginny but Harry has a double nature or shadow
in his scar Horcrux link to Voldemort; his inability to
turn inward and confront this shadow is the cause of

the tragedy at *Phoenix's* end and most of the drama in *Deathly Hallows.*

Like his dad at 15, he was willingly blind to the 'back' of his 'front.' *Deathly Hallows* is largely the story of his coming to terms with his "inner Voldemort,' his purification, and ability to defeat the very real, exterior Dark Lord.

<u>*Magical Creatures*</u>: Double-natured beasties featured in the Hogwarts Gallery include Centaurs, Griffins, Hippogriffs, and the Sphynx with a special mention due to the phoenix, thestral, and unicorn (because they are not what they seem, namely, bird or horse or even bird/horse/dragon).

That so many characters have a twin who is their likeness or antagonistic complement and so many others who live a double existence between worlds makes this aspect of Potterworld – itself divided between Magic and Muggle domains – oddly invisible to many. It's everywhere and consequently "nowhere." I suggest for your consideration that this pairing or unity in division is a central theme of the *Harry Potter* books, that it has an alchemical meaning, and that it is one of the main reasons there are internal resonances, paired letters, and alliteration in so many Potter names.

The activity of alchemy is the chemical marriage of the imbalance ("quarreling couple") of masculine sulphur and feminine quicksilver or mercury. These antipodal qualities have to be reconciled and resolved, 'die' and be 'reborn' after conjunction before recongealing in a perfected golden unity or illumination. Certainly the similarity of this language to the Christian spiritual path is a remarkable one – and understandably so. The symbols of the completion of the alchemical work are also traditional ciphers for Christ, the God/Man, in whose sinless two natures Christians are called to perfection in His mystical body, the Church.

But the end of alchemy is the creation of the Philosopher's Stone which is the transcendence of this imbalance, impurity, and polarity. It is also about the creation of the transcendent alchemist, the saintly God/Man often represented by a Hermaphrodite or "S/He," a person who is both male and female. Here polarity is not resolved as much as it is transcended and embodied in a harmonious unity, an incarnation of love and peace.

Double natured characters — and the list of them is remarkable, no? even Crookshanks is a cross-breed according to Ms. Rowling's web site[28] — are snapshots of the human struggle to resolve in their personal identity the duality of our humanity, our being simultaneously eternal in spirit and ephemeral in the flesh, as images of the God Who is a polarity without duality, a transcendent Absolute and immanent Creator simultaneously. Good guys in Harry Potter embrace this struggle of liminality and strive to incarnate the eternal good; bad guys, as a rule, see themselves as Absolutes above these silly human half-breeds and mudbloods.

On the first point, then, I think, the reduplication of letters and sounds before and within Potter names is a symbol of this alchemical effort human beings make in imitation of the God-Man (and his Virgin-Mother!) to sacrifice self or ego in love for what is greater than one's persona. A character's name, however self-echoing and alliterative, is always about a singular reality, the unity in which we hear the echo, the psychosomatic conjunction of the person as Image of God.

---

28   *http://www.jkrowling.com/textonly/en/extrastuff_view.cfm?id=10*

The second point is similar.

Mirrors are key symbols for understanding Harry Potter because in the first and last books of the series it is how Harry sees himself in the Mirror of Erised and in his godfather's mirror fragment that leads to his victory over the Dark Lord. Ms. Rowling uses the mirror as her symbol of self-understanding, especially with respect to Harry, because of what symbolic role he plays in the books.

In brief, Harry is the "inner heart" or spiritual faculty of the human soul (Ron and Hermione standing in for body and mind). This is the *logos* faculty or conscience, the uncreated aspect of us all, that is, if not the same thing as the Creative Word of God, it is, as C. S. Lewis put it, "continuous with the unknown depth."[29]

In *Philosopher's Stone*, Harry chooses (at age 11!) to go toe-to-toe with Lord Quirrelldemort to do the right thing though it means almost certain death. This sacrificial selfishness and act of heroic love means, as a story symbol for Love himself, he is able to see his own image as he is and is given the Philosopher's Stone, a symbol of eternal life and spiritual riches in Christ. Quirrelldemort is unable to hold him without burning because Harry has identified himself with Love Himself and thereby transcended ego and the World.

In *Deathly Hallows*, Harry looks into a mirror fragment and sees the eye of Dumbledore, a symbol in story both of spiritual wisdom (*gnosis* or the Mind of Christ) and of the "greater I", the transcendent self Harry symbolizes in the story (with a joke about seeing an "eye" where your "I" should be). Harry rejects this reflection and identity at first; the first half of

---

29   Lewis, *Timeless Writings, Inspirational Press, NYC, 1981, page 290* ('The Seeing Eye')

Hallows is his agonizing "struggle to believe." But after his experience with the mirror in the Malfoy Manor dungeon (and Dobby's sacrificial death), Harry dies to his ego persona and rises from his own grave Easter morning having accepted his identity or union with the wisdom in the mirror.

The mirror works in this symbolism because it is the only natural object in which knowing subject and known object are identical. Coleridge and the Romantics, after the Cambridge Platonists and others, believe that the foundation of all knowledge, indeed our capacity to know anything, is in the coincidence of subject and object, i.e., the knowing *logos* within us recognizing its reflection in the *logos* of every created thing and person. This is the relatively esoteric epistemology that is the key to the King's Cross discussion Ms. Rowling says is "the key" passage she waited seventeen years to write, Harry's farewell question to Dumbledore at what he calls King's Cross (see *Deathly Hallows Lectures,* chapter five, for a longer exposition of these ideas).

It is this mirror idea that is at the heart of why Harry's name has two sets of paired letters. His name really has two mirrors in it: Har/ry Pot/ter. Not only does the name literally mean "heir of God," which points to his being an Everyman figure and God's image, but in having these consonantal mirrors we get a picture at the surface of Harry's essential struggle, to identify with his greater Self and transcend ego for union with what is most Real within him.

Alliteration, echoing, and paired or mirrored letters in character names, then, sublimely — "under the threshold" of our conscious understanding — point to the metaphysical themes of the books. The surface reflects the center, nowhere more profoundly than in what is reflected in the surface letters of Ms. Rowling's characters' names.

If you don't see this in Harry James Potter — whose middle name is a signal that he is the image and reflection of his Father and whose last name is assonant with the Latin 'Pater' — then Harry's shadow's names should. Thomas Riddle, Jr., is like Harry the echo or mirror image of his father, both in being a Jr and, by inversion, by his being a Muggle hater as his Muggle father despised magical Merope Gaunt.

But Tom takes the path contrary to the one Harry chooses at his sorting and thenceforth. Tom rejects the challenge of his name, which literally means "twin enigma," a distillation and snapshot of the human challenge as spirit-flesh image of God, to give himself an ego name and identity made from the letters of his given name: Lord Voldemort. In calling his persona 'Lord' he denies he is an image of anything but his time-and-space ephemeral self and in 'Voldemort,' meaning simultaneously both 'flight from death' and 'willing death,' he presents to the world his mission, namely, to become immortal through the murder of others.

If Tom Riddle had understood his given name and struggled to solve the 'twin enigma,' he would have been working on the same path of self-transcendence that Harry Potter, the "Heir of the Potter' or 'Image of God' struggles to walk in *Deathly Hallows*. Both the surface meaning and reduplicated 'd's in 'Riddle' and the internal echoes of **Lord** Voldem**ort**, then, give us the anagogical heart of Harry Potter.

I offer for your considerate reflection (sic), again, that Ms. Rowling's writing is as powerful as it is, not only because of the exciting surface narrative and the postmodern morality confirming our core beliefs, but because of its allegorical portrayal of the human condition and struggle for identity with the Absolute, as well as its relatively sublime artistry and symbolism, alchemical and otherwise. The names, I believe, are no small part of this artistry in that, like the novels themselves, they are comic and engaging at the same time they cue us to and deliver profound meaning.

I covet, as always, your comments and corrections.

CHAPTER 8 --- TRAVIS PRINZI

Loving the Burrow

Understanding the Weasleys as Harry's New Family

W HEN THE POTTER PUNDITS first hit the scene in 2009, I wrote a post for PotterCast.com asking for show topic suggestions. Character studies was the most requested topic in general, and the characters most often suggested were Luna Lovegood and the Weasleys. We've done a show on Luna. This essay is an initial answer to the request for a study on the Weasleys.

The Weasleys become a surrogate family for Harry, the orphan. Summers are always better when he can spend time with the Weasleys. While the magic of Lily's love is invoked over the Dursley household which Harry must call "home," Harry only experiences real love when he's calling the Burrow his home.

The Burrow itself is a fascinating house. While the Wizarding World might call it rather pathetic, being crooked and magically held up and far too small for the large family within, Harry sees it as a beautiful refuge from the mundane repetition of suburbia. On Privet Drive, everything is perfectly manicured, all the lines are straight, all the colors proper. At the Burrow, there is beautiful chaos. But the thing that makes it truly "home" for Harry is that he is loved there. Let's look at the key Weasley characters: Molly, Arthur, Ron, Ginny, Percy, Fred and George.

Mollywobbles and King Arthur

What makes Mrs. Weasley a little crazy is what makes every parent a little crazy: worry about her kids. This is why she's so adamant that Fred and George do well in school. But she's also willing to learn. "They certainly do have a flair for business," she finally admits.

For all of Molly's over-protectiveness, she's a great mom, not least to Harry, who is without a mom. It's in Mrs. Weasley's hugs that Harry finds the kind of warmth that he didn't have growing up and that he can't remember from before he was a year old. Mrs. Weasley is where he finds someone who makes comfort food, cares about his future, and loves him enough to go just a little crazy. I remember well my first reading of *Deathly Hallows*. Mrs. Weasley was acting so incredibly oddly - more so than usual - that I suspected she was Bellatrix on polyjuice. But the oddness of her behavior was all wrapped up on her concern for Harry, Ron and Hermione, who were plotting their quest to destroy Horcruxes.

Of course, the Molly moment everyone remembers best was her attack on Bellatrix LeStrange. "NOT MY DAUGHTER, YOU BITCH!" If you weren't taken by surprise at that moment, there might be something wrong with you. There are at least three surprises here: (1) Neville didn't kill Bellatrix. (2) Molly's use of the word, "Bitch." (3) Molly probably AK'd her.

Concerning the first, I think a lot of us expected that Neville would get his revenge on Bellatrix for torturing his parents into insanity. I'm pretty sure everyone who teared up at St. Mungo's when Neville kept the wrappers was ready for him to take out Bellatrix. We all knew that Harry would get to take out Voldemort. It seemed only right that Neville would get to take out Bellatrix. Somehow, his killing of Nagini just didn't work as a substitute, though I think we've already seen in chapter 4 how Neville was vindicated as a true Gryffindor and a hero. Something just seems a little off about Molly's need to finish off Bellatrix. As students come to her aid, she shouts them back, saying, "Get back! Get *back!* She is mine!" (DH-36) Why? What history do we have of a Molly/Bellatrix rivalry? Certainly the Longbottoms were her friends, but as we've noted, this would create much more of a Neville/Bellatrix showdown. In fact, the only other person who claims "mine" on someone they're trying to kill is Voldemort!

Concerning the second, Molly has just always seemed too proper to shout "BITCH" at anyone. But here's where the Molly vs. Bellatrix thing really works. Bellatrix is not a mother, but she said to Narcissa at Spinner's end that if she had sons, she'd be glad to sacifice them to the Dark Lord's service. She said this knowing full well that Voldemort had sent Draco on a suicide mission. Her love toward Voldemort was demented, and her love for her own children would have been just as deranged. Molly, on the other hand, is a good and loving mother. It was a battle of genuine, persistent love against distorted, unstable love. The love of a mother won out. "'You—will—never—touch—our—children—again!' screamed Mrs. Weasley." And she meant it.

Concerning the third, I'm not entirely sure what to make of Bellatrix's death other than that Molly fired an *Avada Kedavra* at her. "Molly's curse soared beneath Bellatrix's outstretched arm and hit her squarely in the chest, directly over her heart." This curse caused instant death. We have no other curse in the entire series of books that has the same result. Molly used a killing curse. Does this tarnish Molly's reputation? That would require a discussion on unforgivable curses that there is no space for at present.[30] I'll conclude thus: If it was wrong for Molly to use the killing curse, she chose to have a fault at the right time.

Arthur, too, is a model parent. He's a little too lax, some might think, but in a good way, really: he's got a certain fascination about life that he wants his kids to share. Arthur's love of all things Muggle is fascinating. In the same way that we Muggles find the Wizarding World fascinating, so Arthur finds the Muggle world fascinating: eckeltricity, phellytones, and the mystery of flying airplanes. It's the kind of wonder about life most of us have completely lost. How does an airplane stay up? Could we make a car do it? Wouldn't it be great to be able to fly a car to break our friends out of their bad situations? So where Arthur doesn't share Molly's over-protectiveness, his leniency is still founded on an aspect of life his kids need: the desire for adventure.

I think it's safe to say we're all rather glad J.K. Rowling didn't kill off Arthur with that snake attack. For one thing, Sirius's death was enough to deal with

30   I'm of the opinion that the curses are "unforgivable" because the Ministry has proclaimed them so, not because they are worse, by some divine decree, than others. *Confundus,* for example, seems to be a lesser form of the Imperius curse. One can kill a person in other ways besides *Avada Kedavra. Sectumsempra,* for example, can kill and might cause as much or more pain than *Crucio.* This would lead us, then, not to a discussion on the unforgivables, but on the underlying issues: whether it's ever acceptable to kill, even in self-defense.

in Harry's fifth year. But more than that, it *is* nice to
have a consistently good dad all throughout the series.
His flaws are evident enough, but on the whole, he's the
kind of father we probably all want. He's a little quirky,
but not so nutty you're embarrassed by him. He's le-
nient enough to let you have fun, but loves you enough
to risk being unpopular by being firm when necessary.
He's wholeheartedly committed to the good side, rea-
sonable, and trusting. He thinks highly of the kids, and
in that case is very much like Dumbledore. He believes
Harry can handle the knowledge that Sirius Black is
after him, even at 13 years old. He doesn't come down
hard on Harry when he hears the story of the trio's
excursion to Knockturn Alley to follow Draco.

For all that, we never really get Arthur-as-father-
figure the same way we know that Molly is Harry's new
mom. Perhaps that's simply because Molly's mother-
ing is so overt. More likely, it's that motherhood is a
very big deal in the series. We know, of course, that
Rowling was dealing with the death of her mother
when she began writing the series, so great moms
abound in the series. She admitted that she didn't kill
Arthur because there were so few good dads in the series. This is a story about a mother's love, and Molly
ends up standing in Lily's place. Not that Molly could
replace Lily, but she provides Harry with the warmth
of a mother's love that has been lacking in his life
since Lily died. She's not only the anti-Bellatrix, she's
the anti-Petunia. Petunia gives Dudders anything he
wants and screams for, and Dumbledore tells her and
Vernon that they've abused the poor boy by spoiling
him. No such spoiling from Molly! She may seem a
bit too strict, but there's no doubt she loves, and loves
deeply.

One of the most jarring moments in the series is
when Molly can't deal with the boggart, because it

keeps turning into images of her family, dead. In the end, she has to deal with the death of Fred, and that's obviously welling up within her as she attacks Bellatrix. Bella, probably a more talented witch, never stood a chance against Molly's avenging the death of her son.

Fred and George

Fred and George are probably the only two people in history to have engaged in a snowball fight with the Dark Lord Voldemort:

The lake froze solid and the Weasley twins were punished for bewitching several snowballs so that they followed Quirrell around, bouncing off the back of his turban (PS-12).

This is exactly what characters like Fred and George do: use humor and mockery to bring down oppression. They had no idea they were beating Lord Voldemort with their snowballs, but it's a clear pointer to the role the twins play in the series: they're tricksters.

Tricksters are comical characters, but also serve the important role of challenging and toppling oppressive systems. They are full of antics, and they are sometimes perceived as being dumb; in reality, they are more clever than the rest and contribute something fundamental to the plot. The trickster became an important archetype in African American folk tales, for example, serving as challengers to slavery. The trickster defeats the oppressors by outwitting them. S/he is both funny and clever, and shows the oppressor to be a fool.

The trickster twins are nowhere more necessary than in Harry's fifth year. Plunged into the Dark Night of the Soul, CAPSLOCK HARRY is hardly in the place of being a hero. His only attempt to be a hero in this book ends in the death of his godfather, Sirius. While this was an important part of Harry's development, somebody had to take a stand against the oppressive Ministry in the meantime; the tricksters answered the call.

Fred and George are comical through and through, but they are not mere comic relief. They are also thought to be not as intelligent, at least in the mind of Mrs. Weasley; compared to their older brothers, their grades are terrible, and they are always in trouble. It appears they are the classic slackers, caring more about having fun than getting a good education. It turns out that Mrs. Weasley and anyone else who thought that about the Weasley twins were wrong. (We'll return to this in a moment.)

Their rebellion in Order of the Phoenix is classic trickster behavior. Until that moment, Umbridge's tyranny was unchallenged. No one had been able to break her control in the least. From the time of the twins' two-stage rebellion on, Umbridge has entirely lost control. Even the teachers are beginning to revolt, as evidenced by Flitwick's amusing claim that he had to call Umbridge to deal with the Weasleys' magical fireworks in his classroom, because he didn't know if he "had the *authority*" (OP-28).

Consider the attention Rowling pays to her color choices: It's not a coincidence, given the fire theme, that while Harry is off-stage, as far as being the hero is concerned, wrestling with his shadow and in utter darkness and coldness in his soul (the "dark night" or "winter season" of the soul), the red-headed twins launch a rebellion starting with fireworks. Much like Luna lights the way for Harry in his darkness, so bright, red, fiery images play a role in the overthrow of Umbridge's power. The twins make Umbridge look a fool, and she never quite gains control again after the Weasleys' effective revolution against her tyranny.

Fred and George also play a role in vindicating forms of knowledge that don't fit the norm. If Hogwarts were a school under the watchful eye of a Ministry of Magic in the United States, we might imagine that it would be subject to legislation called "No Wizard Left Behind." Hogwarts, especially under the control of Dolores Umbridge, is focused on one thing only: rote memorization of facts in order to pass standardized tests. Mrs. Weasley in particular is agitated that the twins don't follow in the footsteps of Bill, Charlie, and Percy: getting good grades, becoming prefects and head boys, and other such acclamations that are valued by the world of the standardized test. It is believed that only in succeeding in what the government has defined "success" will make one truly successful.

Fred and George throw this out the window. Even Hermione, who clearly thinks books and learning are fundamental to intelligence, is in awe of the brilliant magic Fred and George perform in their joke shop. In the midst of the terror of Voldemort's second rise to power, the most successful business in Diagon Alley is Weasley's Wizard Wheezes. Located just down the street from two shops that the Death Eaters had raided and destroyed, kidnapping their owners, the twins' joke shop mocks Voldemort openly, considering U-NO-POO a much bigger threat.

The Weasley twins disappointed their mother by not getting good grades and dropping out of school. But they weren't dumb; they just didn't fit the dominant discourse about what "counted" as real knowledge. They were more intelligent than Ministry-approved educational curriculum, having created magic that even Umbridge couldn't control. And they were more successful than a good many witches and wizards with all the right test scores and degrees.

Why? They pursued their passion, worked hard at it, and learned what they needed to learn to be successful, regardless of the one-size-fits-all standards. These are successful high-school drop-outs. While I can't recommend dropping out of high school, I can recommend learning from the Weasleys to ask questions about what counts as knowledge.

For the Weasley twins, humor is always the key to getting through every situation, no matter how emotionally complicated. When George's ear is struck with Snape's *Sectumsempra* curse, everyone is huddled around in deep concern. Fred is clearly rattled. George, however, flows seamlessly into humor. He feels "saint-like." Holey. Get it? Holey.

Fred rolls right into it, without a moment's hesitation, telling his injured brother that he's "pathetic" for ignoring the whole world of ear jokes for "holey." What "ear" jokes did Fred have in mind, do you suppose? How should George have responded to the question, "How are you feeling?"

Then we have Fred's death. It seemed to come out of nowhere. Harry was right to reflect that the world had ended. Neither of the twins were supposed to die. Or if one had to, the other should have joined. There's no way these two should have been separated. If the twins are torn apart, the world is torn apart. But Fred died just as the twins should die, if die they must: "with the ghost of his last laugh still etched upon his face" (DH-31).

Is Percy a Slytherin?

Percy wanted to be Barty Crouch, Sr. His power ambitions led him to be complicit with the evil actions of the Ministry of Magic: human rights violations in the form of unjust arrests of innocent people, torture of children in the Hogwarts takeover in book 5, denial of Voldemort's return, and the eventual Nazi-like regime run by Voldemort's puppet, Pius Thicknesse.

J.K. Rowling frequently shows us the way in which an abusive government becomes an ally of the very evil it's trying to prevent by putting them on parallel tracks. The overt racism of the Death Eaters is played out in the racist tendencies to be found within the Ministry: the fountain which told a lie, the Restriction on underage wizardry,[31] the belief that house-elves love slavery, and other similar things. While society on the whole seems to think prejudice is a bad thing ("You mustn't think I'm prejudiced," Slughorn protested), Pureblood racists like the Malfoys still have money and influence, and they still have the ear of the Ministry's policymakers.

Given this, I think we can draw a parallel between Percy and Regulus Black. And even Draco for that matter. Percy is the Ministry parallel of Regulus: he thought he was joining the right side because of a desire for power, and when he got in too deep, he backed out.

Harry's experience with Percy reinforces his being "Dumbledore's man through and through." In fact, Percy was Scrimgeour's ruse for finally getting to talk

31   It's a racist law because by its nature, it can only be enforced on Muggleborns, or in Harry's case, a half-blood living with Muggles. It cannot be enforced on most purebloods and halfbloods, because as magic is always done in those houses, the Ministry can't know that the underage witch or wizard is performing it.

to Harry in *Half-Blood Prince*. The fact that Percy was willing to be used, in a way that would obviously hurt his family, to further his Ministry ambition certainly stood out to Harry. Percy in many ways is an anti-Harry. Harry would rather go it alone in the quest against Voldemort than join forces with the Ministry, so quick to abuse its power. Percy, on the other hand, willingly accepts and repeats the Ministry's lies to achieve a position of power. Only when things got really out of hand did he finally return.

This makes Percy, like so many other characters, more complex than the houses into which they are sorted. One wonders if the Sorting Hat struggled a bit with Percy, because Slytherin would have been a good house for him. But in the end, he made the courageous choice, gave up his Ministry ambitions, and joined the fight against Voldemort. One of the greatest moments of redemption in the series is when Percy says, "Hello, Minister!", then jinxes Thicknesse. "Did I mention I'm resigning?" (DH-31).

Ginny: Does Harry Need a Girlfriend?

Now we come to Harry Potter's girlfriend, a touchy subject no matter how you approach it. To some, she is the wrong choice for Harry. To others, she is the perfect choice. To still others, she might be the right choice, but she just didn't get enough page time for us to know. And yet to others, she could have been the right choice, but Rowling relegates all her power to the sidelines and defines her entirely as Harry's girlfriend instead of her own character.[32] And there's a final group that sees Harry having a girlfriend as too

---

32   See "Ginny Weasley - Girl Next Doormat?" by Gwendolyn Limbach, in *Hog's Head Conversations, Volume 1* (Zossima 2009) for this point of view.

much of a distraction from his own story, particularly the symbolism of it all.

So how do we approach the fiery Ginny Weasley? The same way you'd approach any fire. Carefully. Especially with that bat-bogey hex in her arsenal.

Let's begin with that last group I mentioned above: those who see Ginny as a distraction to Harry's quest. The reasoning is found in the deeper levels of reading the Harry Potter books. The entire series, couched as it is in alchemical imagery, is the story of the formation of the true philosopher's stone: pure-souled Harry. This formation happens in the midst of the quarreling couple: sulfur (Ron) and quicksilver (Hermione). Further, we're dealing here with triptych fiction: the trio represents the human soul - heart, mind, and spirit. Adding a fourth pulls Harry, in his Ginny moments, out of that triptych and into something altogether different.

It's one of the many reasons the Cho story felt like such a distraction *for Harry himself*, if not for the reader. In the darkest book of the series - the nigredo stage of the alchemical work - Harry is isolated. He does not have the warmth of relationship with Ron and Hermione that he usually enjoys. His interactions with Cho completely fall apart; that relationship was never going to work. While Ginny is a better fit for Harry by far, there's still something of a distraction there from Harry's progress toward becoming a true philosopher's stone, which must take place with Ron and Hermione.

This Harry-as-philosopher's-stone reading is also key to understanding how Rowling could stick with *Harry* Potter when she admits to having asked herself the question, "Why not Harriet Potter? Why am I not writing a feminist heroine?" The philosopher's stone is the resolution of contraries, and as such is represented androgynously. Harry, symbolically, is the resolution of male and female. Ginny is a glowing-red reminder that Harry is very male.

I do believe this is the best reading, seeing the deeper-level meaning as foundational to everything else in the series. More Ginny would have been a distraction to Harry's symbol development as a philosopher's stone. Nevertheless, I share with J.K. Rowling the very natural desire to see Harry happy and at peace with a family. Say what you like about the Epilogue, but after everything Harry's been through, it warms the heart to see him standing with Ginny and passing along wisdom to his sons.

And I'm very much of the opinion that if Harry's going to get married, Ginny's the right woman.

Harry's most intimate relationships - his friendship with Ron and Hermione, and his relationship with Ginny, the two most clear-cut anima/animus archetypal sets in the series - are full of fire imagery. Anima and Animus are perhaps the most complex mythological archetypes, but for purposes here, we will make it as simple as possible: the anima is the "feminine side" of a man, and animus is the "masculine side" of a woman. We'll focus primarily on anima as an example, because Harry, our hero, is male. An anima can be a man's idealization of the feminine: everything that he thinks a woman should be. It plays out like this: Harry meets Cho, and she is pretty and appears to be everything that a man is supposed to like in a woman. So he dates Cho, but he simply cannot understand her, her feelings, or her struggles, and as she collapses into a mess of emotions, Harry jumps ship. He has projected his idealized version of the feminine onto Cho, but he has remained just the same person as he always was in relation to her.

On the other hand, Harry begins to feel attraction toward red-headed Ginny. He has matured at this point, and though we know precious little about Ginny, we know this much: she is fiery and she is powerful. These are all things Harry needs, because he has a tendency toward being passive (how much of what happens to Harry in the first six books happens by chance, rather than by active pursuit?). Harry is a bit timid around girls. The whole Cho debacle was a mystifying experience for him. With Ginny, there's no tiptoeing around, no having to guess at what Ginny is feeling. She'll tell you, and she might punch you if she's angry. And she obviously has no problem showing affection and expressing her desires - Harry certainly got his chance to practice his "snogging" technique with Ginny as a girlfriend. The difference between Cho and Ginny is that Cho was a distant projection of the ideal feminine, whereas Ginny and Harry are reconciled to each other through intimate relationship, the drawing of each other toward the "androgyne" middle.

Is Ron a Hufflepuff?

Ron Weasley is afraid of spiders. Who would have expected a kid who's afraid of spiders to be able to stare down Lord Voldemort, who's conjuring images of Harry and Hermione making out, and destroy a bit of his evil soul?

Ron is Harry's best friend, and I think it's safe to say that loyalty is the key attribute here. Ron is loyal to what is good, and loyal to Harry no matter what. Except for the little bit in their fourth year when he got insanely jealous of Harry, and that's precisely because of his greatest weakness - the very thing he had to stare down when facing Locket-crux.

Let's back up a little. From the get-go, we see that Ron and his family are not well-loved by the elite of the Wizarding World. They're the red-headed step-children of the Purebloods. They're poor, not influential, and friends of Muggles.

At the bottom of this family which is already at the bottom of the Wizarding World is Ron Weasley. He's not the youngest, but he's definitely lowest in the popularity ranking, even within the family itself. The youngest, Ginny, is also the only daughter, so she's already one-up on the youngest son. Ron is completely overshadowed by his brothers and their accomplishments.

This is why as he steps in front of that Mirror in his first year at Hogwarts, he sees himself triumphant - Quidditch captain, head boy, and looking good. His desire is to rise above his very low status and get some recognition. This is going to be a problem when your best friend happens to be the Chosen One.

Jealousy blinds Ron to Harry's dangerous plight in their fourth year, and they suffer their first of two serious splits. This first one is remedied quickly enough when Ron observes the peril of the first task and almost loses his friend for good. Ron's problem has not gone away by the time they're on the quest to defeat Voldemort, and the soul-piece in the locket Horcrux takes full advantage of this weakness with which he has yet to deal.

Before the Pool-Mirror

Ron will stand before one more Mirror-symbol, however, and face his greatest struggles and fears head-on. Narcissus (the Greek mythological figure) stood before a pool and was so enamored with himself, he ended up drowning. He couldn't pull himself away from his own reflection. Ron finds himself before a pool, not staring into it, but staring into a sort of distorted Mirror of Erised: the Locket Horcrux is showing him his greatest fears.

> "Least loved, always, by the mother who craved a daughter ... Least loved, now, by the girl who prefers your friend ... Second best, always, eternally overshadowed ... " (DH-19)

It's there in front of this Mirror-symbol that Ron conquers his fears and becomes the kind of person who will no longer see a cover for fear in the Mirror of Erised, but will hopefully see himself alone - or perhaps himself with Hermione. But it would no longer be himself with Hermione because of fear, but because he finds true, deep, lasting contentedness and love with her.

It might be hard to think of Ron as much more than a misplaced Hufflepuff, but the moments we've just looked at solidify his place in Gryffindor. He's a bit of a duffer, sure, but he's a brave duffer. While it remains a bit of a mystery to this reader what the brilliant Hermione Granger ever saw in him, I like Ron. This is not a coward. This is the boy who gave himself up in the journey into the depths of Hogwarts in their first year. From the beginning, Ron was a true Gryffindor, showing courage beyond his years and willingness to die so that Harry could face the thief who was after the Stone. While Ron might have been a part in Dumbledore's chess game, but he's not just a pawn. And we might remember that in Wizard's Chess, the characters have their own voices and movements.

Harry's New Family

New mom and dad, wife, and brothers: the Weasleys represent what home really is, or what it should be. They are happy because they love, regardless of how much money or power or influence they have. This is exactly the right context for Harry. It's interesting and amusingly ironic that the kid with the "hot head" (according to Dumbledore) settles down and is finally at peace with a family of redheads.

Bibliography

Rowling, J.K. *Harry Potter and the Chamber of Secrets.* New York: Scholastic, Inc.,
1999.

Rowling, J.K. *Harry Potter and the Deathly Hallows.* New York: Scholastic, 2007.

Rowling, J.K. *Harry Potter and the Goblet of Fire.* New York: Scholastic, Inc., 2000.

Rowling, J.K. *Harry Potter and the Half-Blood Prince.* New York, Scholastic Inc., 2005.

Rowling, J.K. *Harry Potter and the Order of the Phoenix.* New York: Scholastic, Inc.
2003.

Rowling, J.K. *Harry Potter and the Sorcerer's Stone.* New York: Scholastic, Inc., 1997.

CHAPTER 9 --- JAMES THOMAS

The Omegas in the Alphas

J. K. Rowling's Dazzling Use of Foreshadowing

FORESHADOWING, WHICH CAN BE one of the most complicated and sophisticated of literary devices, can be defined in two words: literary hinting. In most basic terms, if an author foreshadows, she hints here and now that something will be significant later—maybe a page later, or a few hundred pages later, or, in the case of J. K. Rowling, a few thousand pages later.

Foreshadowing is as old as literature itself; from the omens of ancient Greek drama, to Chaucer, to Dante, to Shakespeare, to Jane Austen (Rowling's favorite novelist), casual readers and scholars alike have appreciated and pointed out examples of this literary hinting. The Russian playwright Anton Chekhov once wrote: "If in the first act you have hung a pistol on the wall, then in the following one it should be fired." As we will see, Rowling has hung more than a few pistols on the wall, and by, or in, Book 7 whole arsenals have been fired.

As is the case with talking about literary symbols and themes, foreshadowing is easier to see and more fully appreciated when we are rereading a passage in a literary text, knowing upon re-reading more about the character or action involved than when we first read the passage. For example, we don't really know all the crucial things there are to know about Severus Snape until the fourth chapter from the end of the seventh book; so virtually everything we've read or thought about this magnificent character is altered upon re-reading, since we had no idea what all was being foreshadowed with regard to Snape for 4000 pages.

As we reread Rowling paying special attention to some of the foreshadowed elements, we see that she seems to have a special fondness for and deftness with foreshadowing. I'd like to categorize the foreshadowing in the Potter series in four groups: "fore and aft" foreshadowing or foreaftshadowing, false foreshadowing, ironic foreshadowing, and straightforward or true foreshadowing—fore and aft, false, ironic, and true. None of these kinds of foreshadowing is original with or unique to Rowling, but there are multiple examples of all four in all seven of her novels.

False and ironic foreshadowing understandably would appeal to Rowling because they are misleading and are standard devices of narrative misdirection, the technique of misleading the reader so often employed masterfully by Jane Austen. Readers of *Pride and Prejudice* are quite convinced that Mr. Darcy is " 'orrible," as Fleur might say, before they're convinced he's wonderful—much like the coward and traitor Snape turns out to be "probably the bravest man [Harry] ever knew" (*DH* 758—page references are to the American hardback editions and are cited parenthetically in the text).

Moreover, except in the case of false hints, where the shadows are there but not the substance later, the end is indeed there right for us to see from the beginning. The omegas were present in the alphas all along—as we usually discover only by looking back those few or those few thousands of pages amazed at what all Rowling encoded there. John Granger has called Rowling the "queen of genre busting" for all the literary antecedents and analogues her books remind us of; I'd add that she's the "queen of foreshadowing" as well.

Let's take a look at some examples of each of the four kinds of foreshadowing I have identified in Rowling. First, there's what I call "fore and aft shadowing." In these passages, she mentions something in the present that reminds us of something we encountered in our past reading but didn't realize the full significance of at the time AND she is foreshadowing an upcoming (future) recurrence of this element. Past, present, and future references will eventually yield the whole picture for readers; hence when we come upon the element in the present, it aft-shadows the first occurrence and foreshadows the upcoming occurrence. We find something like this in *Moby-Dick* when Melville focuses our attention on the doubloon from time to time throughout the novel.

In Chapter 11 of *Sorcerer's Stone*, when Hagrid lets the reference to Nicolas Flamel slip (193), Harry is reminded of something and is sure he's read that name somewhere (197). He has, of course, as we re-readers well know. But, at the time, ironically, we first-time readers probably have less of a memory of the name than Harry. I would guess that very few first-time readers turn back to the Hogwarts Express candy-eating spree to look at Harry's Chocolate Frog card again (103); yet the "aft" is there. And so is the "fore" since the mention of Flamel's name and Harry's attempt to recall where he's encountered it are followed by Harry's "eureka" moment as he reads his second Dumbledore card (219).

In *Chamber of Secrets* we have a reference to Peeves's crashing the vanishing cabinet right above Filch's office, thus getting Harry out of trouble (128). This takes us back to an earlier scene in Book 2 when Harry hides from Lucius and Draco Malfoy in the vanishing cabinet at Borgin and Burkes (50), and it takes us forward both to Montague's getting stuck in the Hogwarts cabinet in Book 5 (627) and to Draco's uses of the cabinets in Book 6 to enable Death Eaters to enter the school.

Consider this example of fore and aft shadowing in *Prisoner of Azkaban* during McGonagall's first class of the term. She tells the students what Animagi are, then does her cat/woman routine (108). This takes us back to McGonagall the map-reading cat of Chapter 1 of *Sorcerer's Stone*, complete with the same markings around the cat's eyes to correspond to McGonagall's spectacles, and it gets us ready for the wolf, the rat, the dog, and the stag who used to hang out together in the old days at Hogwarts. Notice that during McGonagall's instruction about Animagi, Harry "hardly heard what Professor McGonagall was telling them . . . " and "wasn't even watching when she transformed herself" into the cat. Anything in the Potter series that seems *that* unimportant must be *really* important a few pages later, as the matter of Animagi surely is.

Another example of a nicely executed fore and aft in Book 3 is when Rowling refers to the kids' Astronomy exam on the "tallest tower" at Hogwarts, thus reminding us of the de-dragoning when Charlie's friends take Norbert (aka Norberta) away in a tower scene in

Book 1—and taking us forward to Sirius's escape from the tower on Buckbeak later in Book 3, to Harry and the others witnessing from the tower Umbridge's first and last trip into the Forbidden Forest in Book 5, and, of course, the towering tower scene ending with the death of the headmaster in Book 6. Big things happen in high places, just like they do in countless other literary locales with serious altitude.

Rowling's casual mention of a bezoar in Book 4 furnishes us another example of fore and aft. Harry is in potions class, but is more interested in asking Cho to the Yule Ball than in brewing his potion properly, so he forgets to add the "key ingredient": a bezoar (396). Re-readers are then led back to Snape's first lesson in Book 1 (when we first hear about bezoars) and forward to Harry's cheeky use of the all-purpose antidote in Slughorn's class, and, soon after, to his saving Ron from the poisoned mead with a bezoar.

In *Order of the Phoenix*, we see fore and aft with Katie Bell. Poor Katie Bell—for a minor character, she's in for some major trouble. She seems randomly targeted by Peeves in Chapter 18 as he hits her with an ink pellet and later empties a whole bottle of ink on her head (377-78). This takes us back to Katie's fate during Quidditch practice (292) when she's accidentally hit in the face by Ron's hard Quaffle pass, and later "helped" by Fred, who makes her nose bleed more not less. Now fast forward to Book 6 where Katie receives a package and thereafter spends more time in St. Mungo's than at Hogwarts.

Notice this very nicely crafted example of fore and aft shadowing in *Half-Blood Prince*. Harry needs, *requires* is the operative word, somewhere to hide his potions book; and when the room appears, now filled with the hidden objects of generations of Hogwarts inhabitants

(526), we remember the D.A. and Dumbledore's night of the full bladder—and we look forward to the room's great significance in Book 7. In fact, we're even told about an old tiara being there among the seemingly worthless junk in the room (527).

Even in Book 7 we find the fore and aft technique, though there's no eighth book for "afts" to manifest themselves in. Early on, when the Dursleys are preparing to leave their house, a confused Dudley, standing "with his mouth slightly ajar," reminds Harry "a little of the giant Grawp" (38). Forgetting the use of the word "little," notice that Rowling takes us back to a mental picture of Hagrid's half bro in Books 5 and 6, and anticipates the role Grawp will play in the Battle of Hogwarts to come. Also in *Deathly Hallows*, consider how Rowling has Harry see Viktor Krum's wand at the wedding and think "Gregorovitch." This takes Harry (and us) back to the name he has heard in a dream early in Book 7, back to the name of the wand-maker he had heard Ollivander use in Book 4—and forward to the role Gregorovitch is about to play in the chapters yet to unfold in Book 7.

Like the fore and aft technique, Rowling uses another device I'll call false foreshadowing throughout the seven books. I don't mean by false foreshadowing quite the same thing as the proverbial "red herring," whereby the author purposefully gives us wrong or insignificant hints. These wrong conclusions we draw ourselves based—at least in part—on how often and how subtly Rowling has made us guess wrong before. So we jump the Chekhov gun and fire away—without a weapon. These are sure-fire (sorry) foreshadowings that turn out to be duds, or Squibs. And sometimes Rowling's proper, by-the-book hinting is of something that just never happens, something we never again come across in the narrative, though we keep a sharp lookout for it (or a sharp listen out for gunfire).

An example of the kind of false foreshadowing I'm talking about would be in William Faulkner's classic short story "A Rose for Emily," when Emily buys a man's nightshirt and a set of men's toiletries with the initials of her beau on them and all the townspeople conclude, "She will marry him." That's a logical conclusion based on the huge hint of the gifts Emily bought. No, Emily didn't buy her lover's gifts to make him more comfortable on the honeymoon; she bought them for him to enjoy for many years after the night she poisons him with arsenic and keeps the corpse in an upstairs room.

In *Sorcerer's Stone,* all Dumbledore sees in the Mirror of Erised is that pair of woolen socks. And perhaps for the entirety of the first six books, we might conclude that's an accurate foreshadowing of one who has led and will continue to lead a life of the mind, philosophically above materialism and life's complexities, and without the deep regrets and foolish desires of most people—a gentleman and a scholar in whom there is no guile our headmaster will continue to be, needing only some more nice socks from time to time. Or so we think.

Consider another example of false foreshadowing: we first see Dumbledore's delicate instruments making strange noises and emitting smoke, sitting on the spindly legged tables in *Chamber of Secrets* (205). Don't you fully expect this to be a major foreshadowing? Don't you just count the pages until we learn what each instrument does and what they reveal to Dumbledore? Yet, they're just there, and Harry smashes them in Book 5, and they're there again (*Reparo*, we assume) in Book 6 even after Dumbledore's death (626), still whirring and puffing but telling us nothing.

First-time readers of Book 3 have told me that Crookshanks seems the animal most capable of evil or of magically transforming into something scary—much more so than poor Scabbers. Crookshanks is smart, all right, and knows a friendly Padfoot to hang out with, but Rowling does at times seem to foreshadow that he's going to be so much more—something like Dean Koontz's Einstein in *Watchers*. I've even had students who tell me they thought Trevor the toad had to be more than just an always lost amphibian. Alas, like Freud's famous cigar, sometimes a cat is just a cat, and a toad is just a toad. And nothing is being foreshadowed here.

Other false foreshadows or, again, things we're convinced are going to be vastly significant but aren't, include, in Book 4, those blasted Blast-Ended Skrewts. Skrewts, despite all they have going for them, have not turned out to be my favorite among the magical creatures in the Potterverse. Of all people, Draco probably says it best (and how often could that sentence and those words apply?) when he says, "What is the *point* of them?" (196). Possible pun on "point," aside, we readers expect and want there to be a point—maybe even a vastly significant one foreshadowed by the fast-growing crusty crustacean-like creatures. Yes, I remember the maze, and we do need the one remaining healthy Skrewt for that gig, but Book 4 might be even better if it were *unscrutable*.

Order of the Phoenix seems to foreshadow one thing clearly with regard to the D. A.: if there's going to be an informer, and surely there is, it's going to be that annoying, skeptical troublemaker Zacharias Smith. He's got to be the snitch, not some long-unnamed friend of pretty Cho's. Also in Book 5, how about this for a sure-fire example of foreshadowing? The depleted and discombobulated Gryffindor Quidditch team's chances of winning the cup this year, Ron says, are about the same "as Dad's got of becoming Minister of Magic" (652). So when Gryffindor pulls the huge upset and wins the cup (702), I'm waiting for Arthur to be visiting the "Other Minister" on Downing Street some day. False advertising, false foreshadowing. I know, technically, Rose and Hugo's grandfather may have become Minister in the nineteen years between the Battle of Hogwarts and the Epilogue, but I'm not believing *that* without seeing it. It's hard to envision the Minister's office with pictures of plugs on the wall.

Lastly, with regard to false foreshadowing, and speaking of the Epilogue to Book 7, much has been written and said about what all isn't addressed in the final pages of *Deathly Hallows*, Arthur's becoming Minister or not being least among them. So, I'll just cite one example: with all the foreshadowing of the kids ending up as Aurors, we get nothing about this or any other occupation they may be engaged in while in their mid-30s. Recall that Rowling said in her NBC interview with Meredith Vieira that Harry is an Auror, but we don't get that and a lot more in writing in the Epilogue. This does not bother me in the least, by the way; I'm not an Epilogue hater. I'm happy with the little that's there, the way it focuses on family life and not on professions. And if Rowling had begun to give us the substance to go with all the unfinished shadows over the four thousands of pages, where would she have stopped? Would she get down to telling us whether or not Mrs. Norris had kittens?

Our third category of Rowling's literary hinting is ironic foreshadowing, the technique whereby something is hinted at, and it happens, but not at all in the way we thought it would happen from the hint provided. In fact, the substance might be quite the opposite of the shadow. An example would be a line in Poe's "Cask of Amontillado." The doomed Fortunato, about to be walled up in the catacombs by his unknown enemy, suffers from a head cold. After a brief coughing spell, he tells his soon-to-be-murderer not to worry about him and says, "I shall not die of a cough." And indeed he will not.

In *Sorcerer's Stone*, as an example of ironic foreshadowing, when Harry overhears intimidating Snape and intimidated Quirrell quarrelling in the forest about an effort to get the stone and about where Quirrell's loyalties lie (226), probably about 99.99% of all first-time readers will read the passage with Snape as villain in mind. It makes perfect sense that way and surely foreshadows that if good Quirrell doesn't come around for the Dark Lord, evil Snape will do him in. Later, when we reread the scene with Quirrell as villain in mind, it makes even more perfect sense (if "more perfect" were possible).

In *Chamber of Secrets* likewise we find ironic foreshadowing nicely misleading us. We have several references to Ginny's very unusual and pronounced reactions to the writing on the wall, the attack on Mrs. Norris, and to other ominous matters going on at Hogwarts during Harry's second year. Ginny's brother Percy says he's never seen her so upset; she's "crying her eyes out" over it all (157). Ron just figures it's all because Ginny is a great cat lover. Wonder why Ginny of all people seems atypically and especially upset by all these things? That's puzzling, isn't it? A real riddle.

In Chapter 13 of *Chamber of Secrets* notice how Ron, who's been polishing trophies for detention, speculates on why the diary owner, "T. M. Riddle," was given the special award for services to Hogwarts. Ron throws out three ludicrous (he thinks) possibilities (232). Notice particularly the order: maybe Riddle got thirty O.W.L.s or saved a professor from the squid in the lake, or "Maybe he murdered Myrtle; that would've done everyone a favor." Silliest possibility of all, isn't it, that model student Tom Riddle would have had anything to do with a girl's death.

We have two excellent examples of ironic foreshadowing in *Prisoner of Azkaban*. The first occurs at the end of Chapter 11 when a very worried Hermione is fearful that the mysterious gift Harry has received is a Trojan broom that has been jinxed, and has told McGonagall about Harry's Firebolt. When a furious Ron turns on Hermione and asks her why she turned on them by turning in the broom, she says, "Because I thought—and Professor McGonagall agrees with me— that that broom was probably sent to Harry by Sirius Black!" (232). Hermione's got the right person, but the wrong reason. The foreshadowing as to the identity of the gift giver is dead-on right, but Hermione couldn't be more wrong about the gift giver's motivations.

Also in Book 3, we have the "unmistakable swish and thud of an axe," followed by a "wild howling" (331-32). Like Ron, Hermione, and Harry, we hear this from a distance, but see nothing with our eyes, but surely nothing could more clearly point to the fact that Buckbeak has been killed and Hagrid is howling in grief. Until we go back in time, and forward about seventy pages, and read, "There was a swishing noise, and the thud of an axe," followed by Hagrid's howls of joy that Buckbeak has escaped (402). In fact, the most significant change in the wording of these two passages is that in the first, "unmistakable" describes the sound of the axe. Is *anything* really unmistakable in Rowling until we read the final word of the final book?

We also find two nice examples of ironic foreshadowing in *Goblet of Fire*. The first occurs when Barty Crouch, Jr., as Mad-Eye seems to be championing Harry, defending him against Karkaroff's insinuations of cheating. The fake Moody seems to express great fear that someone might be out to harm Harry and mentions that only a "skilled" witch or wizard could have put Harry's name into the fire (279), which is quite true since the skilled Barty Crouch, Jr., did just that. First-time readers leave the scene more convinced than ever that even though "Moody" is a maverick, a loose cannon, and, well, moody, he has only Harry's best interest at heart and will protect him through the trials of the tournament, *which he will so his master can then destroy Harry*. The second example of ironic foreshadowing in Book 4 is a bit more subtle. It's when Hermione has been defending Winky, to Ron's displeasure. Sirius then defends Hermione's sympathies for Winky, saying, "If you want to know what a man's like, take a good look at how he treats his inferiors, not his equals" (525). Sounds like good advice, doesn't it? Wonder how Sirius will treat a certain *creature* in Book 5 and with what consequences?

Speaking of *Order of the Phoenix*, how's this for ironic foreshadowing? We discover that Petunia has heard of dementors and knows that they guard the prisoners at Azkaban. Petunia heard "that awful boy" tell "*her*" about dementors (31-32). Harry is at first angry at how his aunt refers to, he thinks, his father and mother. He is then puzzled that Petunia remembered this matter about the magical world. First-time readers probably conclude something is here foreshadowed about the Petunia-Lily-James relationship. Once we've all gotten to "The Prince's Tale" chapter of Book 7, however, we know the "awful boy" of Petunia's memory is young Severus Snape.

With much subtlety, but I believe with deliberate-ness, Rowling ironically foreshadows a future scene, the return of Percy in the Battle of Hogwarts, in the terrible letter he writes Ron in Book 5. Percy's letter of brotherly advice to Ron (296-98) not only confirms our worst suspicions about him and his ambitions and what he wouldn't do to get ahead, but the end of the next-to-last paragraph is interesting from a pro-noun point of view (if, indeed, pronouns are of any interest to you). Percy writes of his parents, "*in time they will realize how mistaken they were and I shall, of course, be ready to accept a full apology when that day comes.*" Now, read Percy's line with a few pronoun substitutions (and verb changes): *in time* I *will realize how mistaken* I was *and* they will, *of course, be ready to accept a full apology when that day comes*"; and *that* day does come, doesn't it? Except the family doesn't even expect or require an apology. And, by the way, I think pronouns are of interest to Rowling. Remember how she lets us think the "he" of Sirius's line "He's at Hogwarts" is Harry instead of Pettigrew for about three hundred pages?

In the early part of *Half-Blood Prince* first-time read-ers think they're getting an unprecedented glimpse of evil Snape's loyalty to the Dark Lord and to his eventu-al murder of Dumbledore. In the Spinner's End scene, one by one Snape deals masterfully with Bellatrix's doubts of his loyalty to Voldemort. And when she asks Snape if Dumbledore still trusts him implicitly, Snape answers, "I have played my part well" (31). And in-deed he *has*; in fact, he *is* playing his part well face to face with Bellatrix. So, still further, when he takes the Unbreakable Vow with a "blank" and "unreadable" expression on his face (35), Snape promises in Chapter 2 of *Half-Blood Prince* to do what he does in Chapter 27. We thus think we have straightforward foreshad-owing of evil Snape's most heinous act; we think this for two years until Book 7 shows us how ironic the foreshadowing in Book 6 indeed is.

Two examples of ironic foreshadowing in Book 7 both involve Mad-Eye Moody. One is apparently ironic to readers at the time, for Mad-Eye, probably a bit proud of the "Seven Potters" escape plan using the decoys, says, "Even You-Know-Who can't split himself into seven" (50). In the spirit of Maxwell Smart, would you believe eight, Mad-Eye? A bit later, just as the pairs with the real and the fake Harrys are about to embark, it's Mad-Eye, of all people, who says, "See you all in about an hour at the Burrow" (55).

The fourth category of Rowling's foreshadows is the largest group, so I've been most selective in looking at a few examples from each of the books. This category is the traditional straightforward, or true, foreshadowing, whereby what is hinted at *does* come to pass and in the same way we think it will. Here's an example: remember in *The Great Gatsby* when we have a minor automobile mishap early on in Gatsby's driveway, and later when we have references to Jordan's bad driving and Nick's comments to Jordan that she's a "rotten driver"? It sounds to me like someone in this careless crowd is surely going to have a deadly accident before that story's over.

Two quick examples from *Sorcerer's Stone* of true foreshadowing occur in the first chapter. Arguably the most famous early casual name dropping that turns out to be a center-stage matter later in the whole Potter series may be Hagrid's comment that he's borrowed young Sirius Black's motorcycle to bring baby Harry to the Dursleys. In case you've forgotten, this comment is made fourteen pages into the 4100 page saga. Even earlier in Chapter 1 of Book 1, McGonagall predicts that Harry will be famous, will be a legend, and that "there will be books written about Harry" (13). Clearly, McGonagall is thinking of Harry's legendary role in the Wizarding world (she goes on to say that "every child in our world will know his name"). Keeping her predictions within the Wizarding world, we find here an example of true foreshadowing. Applying her words to the Muggle reading world, we find rich ironic foreshadowing as well, for there will be books written about Harry and annual conferences to discuss his saga; and just about every Muggle child and adult knows his name.

What an intriguing foreshadow we find in the dream Harry dreams his first night at Hogwarts. Only a few days after he has met Draco Malfoy and only hours after he has first seen the turbaned Quirrell and felt the cold stare of Snape, Harry dreams that he is wearing the turban, which is telling him he must become a Slytherin and which becomes increasingly heavy and painfully tight (130). As Harry tries to remove the turban, Draco laughs at him, turns into Snape, who laughs with a "high and cold" laugh—then "there was a burst of green light and Harry woke, sweating and shaking." That's quite a dream. It not only foreshadows the ominous true nature of the turban and events to come later in Book 1; it also indicates how much Rowling may have already planned for the events of the future books. In a sense Draco, the would-be killer of Dumbledore, will turn into Snape from whose wand comes the burst of green light that night on the Astronomy tower many hundreds of pages later, as Harry's mentor is lost and his nightmare comes true.

The scene in *Sorcerer's Stone* of Harry's first lesson with Snape (137-38) is one of the most impressive and important passages foreshadowing future events in the entire Potter series. Rowling structures this first Potions lesson and Snape's cruel questioning and intimidation of Harry masterfully. Snape poses three questions, to which Harry has no answers. He asks what the addition of asphodel to wormwood produces, which is the Draught of Living Death; he asks where a bezoar can be obtained, which is from a goat's stomach; and finally he asks the "difference" between monkshood and wolfsbane. In fact, this last question is one of those proverbial professorial "trick" questions since monkshood and wolfsbane are the same plant. Yet it seems that Rowling has more in mind than just letting us see Snape intellectually bludgeoning Harry in the present. Rowling has given us three props she will use in the future as well, or three more Chekhov guns that are sure to go off later. A Draught of the Living Death is reminiscent of what Snape gives Dumbledore to enable him to live another year, and, in an even closer parallel to future books, Snape has just told the class that one who masters Potions can "even stopper death" (137). The bezoar, as we've already mentioned, will turn up again in the Half-Blood Prince's annotated text and will save Ron's life in Book 6. And "wolfsbane"? Well, lucky for everyone that Snape will brew up a nice smoldering batch every month for a Hogwarts werewolf colleague who might otherwise grow hostile (and hairy).

In *Chamber of Secrets*, during Harry's first trip to Dumbledore's office, we have a really rich foreshadowing of Fawkes's role in the last part of Book 2, as the headmaster tells Harry that phoenixes can "carry immensely heavy loads, their tears have healing powers, and they make highly *faithful* pets" (207). In reverse order, Fawkes will come when Harry demonstrates he is faithful and loyal to Dumbledore; his tears will heal Harry's wound; and he will take Harry, Ron, Ginny, and He-Who-Used-To-Be-Lockhart up the long tunnel to safety. Also in Book 2, when the kids are choosing their courses for third year, long before we get all the obvious foreshadows that Hermione is doing the impossible in Book 3 and taking classes simultaneously with each other, and long before we know what a Time-Turner is, we get this innocuous sounding one-liner: "Hermione took nobody's advice but signed up for everything" (252).

In *Prisoner of Azkaban*, the cumulative effect of the slight and brief foreshadows involving Scabbers is impressive. The rat is in the Weasley family photo that makes the paper (9); he's losing weight and his whiskers are drooping (57); he has a missing toe (59); and he's lived far beyond the life expectancy of an ordinary rat (59). We must conclude that this is no ordinary rat, and we might indeed conclude just that even before Crookshanks comes on the scene or Scabbers goes into hiding at Hagrid's. The operative meaning of a "rat" in *Webster's Collegiate* here is "a contemptible person . . . one who betrays or desserts friends . . . ." The dictionary lists as a synonym "scab," one meaning of which is "a contemptible person." Scabbers was well named all along.

Another example of character being foreshadowed nicely is in regard to Rowling's treatment of Cedric Diggory. He's introduced in Book 3, where he wants a rematch even though his team won, because Harry fell off his broom during the Quidditch match (180). Later he congratulates Harry on his new Firebolt (257), and in Book 4 he reminds his own father that he defeated Harry by accident rather than by superior play (72). Cedric also seems to be responsible for Harry's being persecuted less for being the second competing champion from Hogwarts in the Triwizard tournament. This kind of integrity and nobility of character are typical of Rowling's portraits of Cedric. The only exception is when Harry undergoes character assassinations of Cedric in his mind, based not in reality but on Cedric as successful suitor of Cho. All this pre-pares us for Cedric's "noble" behavior during the tour-nament, up to and including his actions in the maze, where the nobility of his character will be consistent until the moment of his death.

We have a clear example of a character's very nature and personality foreshadowing his death in the case of Fred Weasley. Fred, from the time he first hears about the seventeen-year-old requirement for the Triwizards champions in *Goblet of Fire*, begins working on a way to compete. When Hermione reminds him that peo-ple have died in earlier competitions, Fred says, "Yeah . . . but that was years ago, wasn't it? Anyway, where's the fun without a bit of risk?" (190). So, not surpris-ingly, Fred is the first to try to enter his name; he's the first to sign up for the D.A. in Book 5; and he's among the first casualties in the Battle of Hogwarts.

In *Goblet of Fire*, just after the champions have completed the second task, Rowling provides us with another key foreshadowing element, this time with re-gard to the stunningly beautiful Fleur Delacour. We learn here that Fleur "had many cuts on her face and arms and her robes were torn, but she didn't seem to care, nor would she allow Madam Pomfrey to clean them" (505). She then directs Madam Pomfrey to look after her sister and formally thanks Harry and Ron for their rescue of the girl. For a character presented to us initially as vain or at least quite conscious of her extraordinary appearance, Fleur clearly shows here a concern for the well being of others over herself; and she emerges as one for whom some things are more important than good looks.

Consider all this in light of the scene in the hospital wing in Book 6 when Bill has been mauled. Fleur's character and her priorities in the lake scene precisely foreshadow her reactions to Molly's assumption that the wedding is off. In fact, if we look back at some of the phrases describing Fleur after the trial in the lake, with the werewolf attack on Bill in mind, notice we have "had many cuts . . ." on the "face," "but she didn't seem to care, nor would she allow,"—there she would not allow Madam Pomfrey to clean her wounds, and here she will not allow Molly Weasley to put the ointment on Bill. To resort to the old cliché, there's more than meets the eye with regard to Fleur; it's just that it's hard to see that because so much meets the eye. The scene in *Goblet of Fire* foreshadows the development of a character who is much more than fluff and quite undeserving of "phlegm."

When Molly Weasley embraces Harry in *Goblet of Fire*, realizing the ordeals he's been through and sensing that Harry blames himself for Cedric's death, Rowling writes that Molly "bent down, and put her arms around Harry. He had no memory of ever being hugged like this, as though by a mother" (714). This is not only one of the more tender scenes in the entire series; it foreshadows how Harry will become Molly's seventh son. Recall that in the next book, he goes into Arthur's room at St. Mungo's as a family member and becomes increasingly like a Weasley son from this moment on. By the way, at any given time from here on out, Molly essentially has six sons, in a way, since Harry's becoming like her own coincides with Percy's estrangement in Book 5, and Percy's return is followed quite soon by Fred's death in Book 7.

As we move now to *Order of the Phoenix*, we again find many examples of straightforward foreshadowing. As Harry and the others first enter number twelve Grimmauld Place, "it was as though they had just entered the house of a dying person" (60). This is not merely a comment on the depressing nature of the place since the heir to the house of Black is doomed to pass through the veil at the Ministry by book's end. The all-important locket of Book 6 is mentioned, barely we might point out, in Book 5 as well. Rowling "buries" the locket in a paragraph describing items Harry and the others come upon when cleaning out cabinets at Grimmauld Place. Five items are mentioned there, in this order: a kind of "many-legged pair of tweezers," a musical box with Binns-like soporific effects, *the un-openable locket*, a number of ancient seals, and an Order of Merlin, First Class (116). The locket seems the least significant of the items, mentioned casually in the middle of a casual list of house of Black "stuff," clutter, junk items; but there it is, waiting for someone to unlock its secrets.

As early as Chapter 12 of *Order of the Phoenix*, Fred and George have indicated they'll be leaving Hogwarts before completing their education there. As Fred says, "we feel our futures lie outside the world of academic achievement" (227). Of course, with their inventions and preparations for the joke shop, their departure is even more heavily foreshadowed. A little more subtle, though, is the twins' invention and demonstration of the Headless Hats (540), suggestive maybe that they're not intellectual, they'll no longer be under the headmaster at Hogwarts, or that they'll not be using their heads to study for N.E.W.T.s in the future. More ominously, note that it is Fred who demonstrates the hat; he puts it on, smiles, and after only a second "both hat and head vanished"—somewhat reminiscent of the final instant of Fred's life two years later, as he dies with a trace of a smile still on his face.

What an extraordinary example we have of foreshadowing in Book 5 when Harry snaps at Snape (and Snape snaps back) during one of the Occlumency lessons. Trying to get Harry to learn to close his mind,

Snape tells him that it is not Harry's job to know what Voldemort is saying to his Death Eaters. Harry's response is, "No—that's your job, isn't it?" (591). Instead of answering in anger, Snape, after "a long moment" responds with "a curious, almost satisfied expression" and with "his eyes glinting," says, "Yes, Potter . . . That is my job."

Harry seems to assume his supreme insult, tantamount to calling Snape a Death Eater still in league with the Dark Lord, will be met with rage. Snape's extraordinary reaction is explicable only when we re-readers know that Harry has just described Snape's vital and dangerous role as a double agent. You might even say Harry has, quite unwittingly, paid his most hated professor a compliment. Unknown and unintended though Harry's comment is, this would-be insult is, in fact, probably the only nice thing Harry ever says to Snape during his lifetime.

When we examine *Half-Blood Prince* for foreshadowing, we notice that in an early and in a late scene in the book, Harry finds himself, very much against his will and to his frustration, invisible and immobilized. Draco, involved in both scenes, screams *Petrificus Totalus* in the compartment of the Hogwarts Express to harm and humiliate Harry; and Dumbledore wordlessly immobilizes an invisible Harry on the tower to protect him (153, 584).

When Harry and Dumbledore are in the cave and the headmaster is drinking off the twelve goblets of the potion, Harry hates what he has to do: make Dumbledore keep on drinking; yet Harry has promised to do so. "Hating himself, repulsed by what he was doing," Harry keeps forcing down goblet after goblet, according to his promise (571). This foreshadows what Snape does on the tower later that night. As

Dumbledore says "Severus . . . please," there is "re-vulsion and hatred" in Snape's face (595). Knowing now what we know about that plea from Dumbledore and the promise Snape has made, we see how Harry's agony at seeing Dumbledore suffer as a result of *his* promise strongly foreshadows Snape's agony at seeing Dumbledore's life end as a result of his.

In *Deathly Hallows* Rowling might be using a little number foreshadowing. She's said on many occasions that math is not her strength, but we can all count to thirteen when we have to. What I refer to is that on that fateful night when the seven Potters and their escorts take to the skies, thirteen people come to the Dursleys' house to rescue Harry (45). Moreover, af-ter the return of all who do return to the Burrow, we have another group of thirteen. Dung has defected, Mad-Eye is dead, and Kingsley has had to go to work; Ginny and Molly are now added to the group, making a total of thirteen who raise their glasses in Bill's toast to Mad-Eye (79). Two groups of thirteen on a night fraught with loss and with many losses yet to come is something that Sybill Trelawney and I can't help but think isn't accidental.

Griphook's eventual behavior is foreshadowed in Book 7, in spite of readers' conclusions that perhaps, as with Kreacher later, Harry's goodness has trans-formed the goblin. Griphook's lying about the sword being a fake and his being impressed at Harry's burial of Dobby reinforce this idea. But Bill, who knows gob-lins the best, turns out to furnish us with the real hint-ing that Griphook will take the sword in the end, as he tells Harry: "If you have struck any kind of bargain with Griphook, and most particularly if that bargain involves treasure, you must be exceptionally careful" (516).

I'd like to close with two rather impressive examples of foreshadowing, both of them straightforward—one is noteworthy for how beautifully a sad moment is foreshadowed by earlier scenes, and the other is perhaps the earliest hint we have in Book 1 as to how things are going to turn out in Book 7.

The first has to do with Colin Creevey. Colin's death in Book 7 is, it seems to me, strongly foreshadowed in Book 2. In *Chamber of Secrets*, just after Harry talks with Dobby in the hospital wing, Dumbledore and McGonagall bring in the petrified body of Colin. McGonagall has found him "trying to sneak up here to visit Potter" (180). When Harry overhears this, his "stomach gave a horrible lurch." The description of Colin's *death* in Book 7 is strikingly similar. Harry sees the body of Colin, again borne by two people, Neville and Oliver Wood, being taken to the Great Hall with the others killed in the Battle of Hogwarts. Harry "felt another dull blow to his stomach": Colin Creevey, though underage, "must have sneaked back" to fight in the battle (694).

The parallels are indeed close; taken together, they show not only the care Rowling takes in her narrative voice, but also the consistency of Colin's character. He is under-aged and undersized for what his heart tells him to do, and he twice pays a price for his considerable courage. The crucial difference in the two very similar scenes is simple and profound. In Book 2, in the end, when the Mandrakes are ready, Colin, Hermione, and all the others who've been petrified are returned to normal; but in Book 7 no Mandragora, no magic of any kind, can bring Colin back. "He was tiny in death."

I suspect that Rowling structures even another passage, many pages earlier in *Chamber of Secrets*, at least in part, as a foreshadowing of tiny Colin's eventual fate. The scene takes place in a crowded hallway after classes are over and students are rushing to dinner. Harry, with Ron and Hermione, walks along, preoccupied about another matter, and as they pass Colin, he, predictably, says an enthusiastic, "Hiya, Harry!" (153). Harry says hello back "automatically," but before Colin can finish a sentence, he's lost in the crowd. Since Colin "was so small he couldn't fight against the tide of people bearing him toward the Great Hall; they heard him squeak, 'See you, Harry!' and he was gone." As we did with the passage involving Fleur after the trial in the lake, we look here at certain phrases again and are struck by Rowling's artistry in foreshadowing, phrases like "so small he couldn't fight against the tide . . . people bearing him toward the Great Hall . . . and he was gone."

In the title and in the closing line of Chapter 1 of Book 1, with its Dickensian, orphan-on-the-door-step scene, is the phrase "the boy who lived." Here, in these four words which occur well over four thousand pages before we know Harry's fate, Rowling, the queen of foreshadowing, provides us with quite a clue as to whether Harry will live or die at the conclusion of the series. There it is, plain to see looking back now, knowing what we know. Just by a little tweaking of verb tenses, we have our foreshadow of the end of Harry's story given to us at the beginning; for "the boy who lived!" is going to be the boy who *lives*, and love—just love—is going to make all the difference and make all good things possible. All that guessing and all those predictions, especially in the two years between Books 6 and 7, and all we needed was a little verb tense tweaking.

In case this sounds too simple or too unlikely, that "lived" foreshadows "lives," that Rowling would be that conscious or aware of verb tenses, consider a parallel in the dedication of *Sorcerer's Stone*. In addition to her sister Di who heard Harry's story first, Rowling dedicates Book 1 to her late mother Anne who "loved" stories and to her daughter Jessica "who loves stories." As with the dozens and dozens of foreshadowed elements throughout Rowling's books, maybe the omega of Harry's fate *was* right there in the alpha. So, all along, we should have known that he who lived would be he who lives, and that we of little faith needn't have worried that in the end all would be well.

CHAPTER 10 --- JOHN GRANGER

Why She Chose 1692

The Real World Referents of Seekers and Muggles

An edited transcript of John Granger's second talk at the Infinitus Harry Potter Conference Orlando, Florida, 16 July 2010.

G OOD AFTERNOON! THIS AFTERNOON'S talk represents something completely different for me. If you were at my morning talk, you know my job as Potter Pundit is to explain the popularity of the Hogwarts Saga by laying out the artistry and meaning of those books.

That work is a lot of fun; I really enjoy talking about the literary keys that unlock the world's best-selling books. The care with which they were written – the literary alchemy, ring composition, and profound symbolism – reward careful reading and research. Not to mention the opportunity Potter Punditry creates for me to talk with folks like you!

This afternoon, though, I want to explore something more historical than literary, a puzzle or mystery evident in many seemingly unrelated pieces and details of the books. Working from the date of the International Statue of Wizarding Secrecy – 1692 – and a bunch of data from Harry Potter canon, I want to argue that the witches and wizards of our favorite books come from a *'real world'* Christian sect that all but disappeared at the end of the 17th Century.

This talk, of course, is laughably speculative. My best guess is simultaneously non-verifiable and impossible to be proven wrong, barring a remarkable change of heart on Ms. Rowling's part and her speaking openly about such things. For those of you who miss the days of speculation and intelligent guesswork before Deathly Hallows was published, however, this promises to be a fun flashback.

Just to keep this speculation from wandering all over the map, I will start with a statement of my premises, the questions I hope to answer, and my working thesis.

My first premise is that Joanne Rowling is remarkably attentive to detail in her stories, especially with respect to names and sequences, and that there is meaning in these details.

My second premise is that the International Statute of Wizard Secrecy marks the defining moment in Muggle/wizard relations. The legislative and binding agreement to separate from non-magical peoples established the boundaries and parameters of wizarding existence from that time forward.

My conclusion from these two premises is that the choice of 1692 is meaningful, by which I mean that it was not a date chosen arbitrarily or coincidentally.

My three questions from this foundation are: Why 1692? What does this date tell us about wizards, especially those in the UK? Does this information help us understand Harry Potter more meaningfully?

My thesis is this: The end of the 17th Century in England is the time at which a specific sect of Christian believers – the hermetic spiritualist group pursuing human perfection known as the Seekers – disappeared. The beliefs of this sect are in large part the implicit message of the Hogwarts Saga.

The Florence Connection

I have to start my speculation about 17th century English wizards in a place far, far from England and a time well before 1692. To lay the foundation for my argument, I want to go to a place and a time I can be reasonably sure are important to the Potter books – Renaissance Italy, and specifically the Florence of Dante, Ficino and Pico Della Mirandola.

The Potter connections with Florence are remarkable both in their number and quality. Let's start with the most obvious: Firenze the Centaur. "Firenze" is the Italian word for Florence – and we get a touch right away of what Ms. Rowling thinks is important about Florence in this centaur's being both an astrologer and one who doesn't believe the stars predestine fate.

Maybe you don't like centaurs – how about Hippogriffs? These magical flying creatures are taken straight from the 16th Century *Orlando* epics by

Boiardo and Ariosto, the modern world's first heroic, fantasy fiction work.

If you have read anything I've written or are familiar with Ms. Rowling's 1998 interview in which she was asked if she ever wanted to be a witch, you know that *literary alchemy* is the "internal logic" of the series and sets the magical parameters of Harry's world. Alchemy comes to the West through Ficino's translations of *Hermes Trismegistos* and Ficino's incorporation of alchemical perfectionism into Christian Doctrine with Pico, Bruno and others. Alchemy is a huge part of Harry Potter – and it comes out of Renaissance Florence.

Hogwarts is a school of Four Warring Houses that have the qualities of the Four Elements – they are also historical ciphers for the four warring cities of Renaissance Italy: Florence, Naples, Venice and Milan. More to the point, Florence itself is a city historically separated into four quarters:

> The historic centre of Florence is traditionally divided into four quarters, named after the most important churches. Three of them are on the right-hand bank of the Arno, "di qua d'Arno": Santa Maria Novella, which has a red gonfalon decorated with a gold sun on a sky-blue ground; San Giovanni, which has a green gonfalon with a temple (the Baptistery, dedicated to Saint John) on a sky-blue ground; and the quarter of Santa Croce, which has a sky-blue gonfalon decorated with a gold cross. The only quarter "di là d'Arno" is Santo Spirito, which has a white gonfalon emblazoned with a dove.[33]

33　　　*http://www.firenzeturismo.it/en/find-out-more/15-storia/370-curiosita.html*

I think, too, that the primary divide in the Wizarding World – the age old battle between the students of Godric Gryffindor and Salazar Slytherin – is mirrored in the Florentine civil war between Guelphs and Ghibellines.

Which brings us to Dante and his *Commedia*, the epic *Divine Comedy*. The Bard of Florence is a Rowling favorite, clearly, as explained in chapter 4 of *The Deathly Hallows Lectures*, because of her lifting Snape's death scene and Lily's green eyes straight from the end of the *Purgatorio* and the Epilogue names from Dante's beatific vision of a celestial white rose. The conjunction of *Albus* Potter, whose first name means "white," and *Rose* Weasley on Platform 9 ¾ at the saga's finish is not an accident.

If you take away one thing from Florence, though, and why Ms. Rowling points to it, let it be the hermetic or esoteric work of Marsilio Ficino and Giovanni Pico Della Mirandola. They created a synthesis of mystical Christianity from the Orthodox East, Cabala studies from Spanish Judaism, and occult sciences – alchemy, astrology, and memory -- from the Levant that promised a way to divinization or human perfection by manipulation of the sacred order of nature.

In the view of these Renaissance Christians in Florence (like Ms. Rowling's centaur, Firenze), man was not subject to fate or destiny but could exercise choice and ignite the life and light within him to become divine himself. This esoteric alternative to orthodox, passive, and devotional Christian faith is important historically because this Florentine Christian perfectionism spreads across Europe and becomes an engine driving what is known as "the Radical Reformation."

A Little History:
The Reformation and 17ᵗʰ Century England

How do we get from the court of the Medici in Renaissance Florence to the International Statute of Wizarding Secrecy in 1692? In a word, the Reformation. Forgive me here, but to make the connections I need to between Harry Potter canon details and the real world of 1692, I'm going to have to review one point of theology and at least one century of history. It's pretty straightforward, I promise, and the payoff is fascinating – to me at least!

The theological point is the heart of the Protestant Reformation, namely, *primitivism*. The church reformers fought for a return to the ancient, uncorrupted, primitive church of the Apostles which they believed Rome had left behind with its church and …. Innovations. There were three degrees of Primitivism historians have labeled conservative, liberal, and radical.

The "conservative" or Magisterial Reformation – what we call Anglicans, Presbyterians, and Lutherans – felt that the primitive church could be restored relatively easily by returning to Scripture and throwing off the Papacy.

The relatively "liberal" reformers were Puritans and pietists who weren't satisfied with these changes, if they did choose to live in passive obedience to secular and ecclesiastic authority. They wanted a separation between church and state for a return to the primitive church they imagined that was "in the world but not of the world."

The Radical Reformers, in contrast with the liberal and conservative Protestants of the time, pursued the ultimate in primitivism; they believed there was no possibility of restoring the true church because it had deviated so far from its divine origins. These radical primitivists were known as "Seekers" because they sought - and could not find – the true church.

There were two types of Seekers, neither of which resembles the "spiritual, not religious" folks or "rootless inquirers" we describe with that word today.

The first type of Seeker believed that they must wait for God to restore His primitive Church in a new revelation or dispensation. Their longing for a new "word of God" makes historians call them "Literal Seekers." We call these sort of Seekers "Mormons" and "Disciples of Christ" today because their churches were formed in the 19th Century around remnants of the literal Seekers who survived and thrived in North America. The golden plates revelation of the Latter-day Saint prophet, Joseph Smith, Jr., was the fulfillment of the literal Seekers' expectation.

The second type of Seekers, the so-called Spiritual Seekers, believed that there would be no restoration of an exterior church reality; the second coming of Christ to them was not a newer Testament or church denomination, but the realization of the light and life of Christ within the individual believer. They had no rituals, no clergy, no creeds, no sacraments; they believed in individual perfection in Christ.

The Italian and German students of Florentine Christian hermeticism -- most notably Cornelius Agrippa, Paracelsus, and Jakob Bohme, whom you recall from your chocolate frog cards no doubt – become the guiding lights of these spiritual seekers and radical non-conformists pursuing perfection outside of church mysteries and ritual. The magical Christianity of

Renaissance Florence that existed within Catholicism during Dante, Ficino, and Pico's times, when it travels north during the break up of Catholicism in the Reformation, becomes the perfectionist vision of the Spiritual Seekers.

And for a short period of time – the Commonwealth and Protectorate Periods after the English Civil War – it seemed, again, just for a moment, that these Seekers, the Christian hermetic magi, might win the day.

Which brings us to 17th Century England.

1692: Beginning the End of the English Nightmare

You have your score card now of all the players on the pitch in the nightmare of 17th century England, the gory 1600s, a nightmare we've got to review, of course, if we're going to understand 1692 and why wizards went underground then. We've got conservative Reformers who just want to get rid of the Pope, we've got liberal Reformers who want a separation between the church and the world, and we've got the radical Reformers who think "reform" of the church isn't possible. The literal Seekers are waiting for a "new revelation" or dispensation and the spiritual Seekers have turned inward in pursuit of a hermetic human perfection outside the church.

Let's hit the high points of the century and see how our four players fare.

As the century begins, England is a Protestant nation experiencing a Renaissance of arts, business and culture under Queen Elizabeth I.

Elizabeth dies in 1603, however, and James I ascends the thrones of both England and Scotland. He dies in 1625 and Charles I becomes king. He pushes the prerogatives of the King so far as head of Church and State, however, that Civil War breaks out and rages for the better part of a decade: 1642-1651. Charles I is beheaded by act of Parliament in 1649.

The several Civil Wars – there are different ways of counting the distinct wars between groups of Royalists and Reformers in England, Scotland, and Ireland – are responsible for the deaths of hundreds of thousands of soldiers and civilians by disease, dislocation, and actual battle. A contemporary demographer estimated that more than 40% of Ireland died or emigrated in this period, the *de facto* genesis of the Catholic-Protestant divide there.[34]

The Protestant Roundheads – so-called because of their distinctive bowler haircuts – under Oliver Cromwell rule the land as a Commonwealth and a Protectorate until 1660 when Charles II becomes King in what is called the Restoration. But the restoration of the monarchy, a King who heads the State Church, doesn't happen without opposition. A group of Fifth Monarchy Non-Conformists rebel in Venner's Rising (1661) and Charles II both crushes the rebellion and passes a series of acts to repress the radical sects and the Catholics. Notably --

- **Corporation Act** (1661): Receiving Communion within the Church of England is required of all elected officers and agents of government, which effectively excludes Catholics and non-conformists from political power;
- **Act of Uniformity** (1662): Required use of the *Book of Common Prayer* during worship services and Anglican ordination of all clergymen;

---

34   Carlton, Charles (1992), *The Experience of the British Civil Wars*, London: Routledge, pages 212-214

- **Conventicle Act** (1664): Prohibition of unlicensed gatherings of more than five people to repress Catholic and non-conformist worship;
- **Five Mile Act** (1665): Prohibition of non-conformist preachers living within five miles of towns and cities;
- **Test Acts** (1672,1678): Requirements of proof that officials of state do not believe in Catholic ideas of transubstantiation in the Eucharist.

[A curious aside: along with non-conformist sects like our Spiritual Seekers, Catholicism was effectively repressed in the United Kingdom until the Catholic Relief Act of 1829, passed largely through the support of the Duke of Wellington, Arthur Wellesley. Arthur Weasley, Muggle lover and blood traitor, is probably named for the Victor at Waterloo and seeming sympathizer with Catholics.]

Because of this repressive legislation, then, of our four Protestant players on the United Kingdom's stage, only the conservative Reformers, the regime Church of England, are doing well.

Actually, though, no one does well in 17th Century England except the grave-digger and undertaker. If you find a time machine in your grandfather's attic and you only have one time and place you can visit, I'm thinking Mao's Cultural Revolution, WWI's trenches, and the United Kingdom in the 1600s are competing for the top destination to which you *don't* want to go. The mayhem and chaos of the English Civil Wars are just the beginning of the 17th Century nightmare in the UK.

The Reign of Charles II is marked first by the Great Plague (1665-66), in which pestilence about 10% of the nation dies, and then by the Great Fire of London in 1666 that destroys the greatest city in the realm. If this weren't enough, though, Charles II dies without children so James II takes the throne, a king who is a secret, then not-so-secret Catholic. When his Catholic wife gives birth to a son and James tries to loosen laws against Catholics (Declaration of Indulgence, 1687), he is expelled from the throne. 1688 finds William II as the king after what is known as the "Glorious Revolution." William's priority, of course, as the head of the Church of England is further repression of the non-confirmists and Catholics.

The Spiritual Seekers:
A Tale of Three Brothers and John Everard

What were our perfectionist and radical primitivist friends, the spiritual Seekers, doing during this century of political upheaval and religious persecution? In a nutshell, they arrive on the scene just before Elizabeth's death at the height of the Rosicrucian Renaissance, Shakespeare's London, they surge in numbers and influence during the Civil Wars, and they are brutally put down at century's end. At the dawn, peak, and fall of the Seekers in the 1600s we find a curious Harry Potter pointer and echo.

The first is from the *Tales of Beedle the Bard* and specifically the tale which makes up a large part of the back story in *Deathly Hallows,* namely, 'The Tale of the Three Brothers.' The ideas of the German radical reformation and of the Florentine hermeticists which are the core beliefs of the Spiritual Seekers came to England in the 1590's through the labors of Three Brothers – Walter, Thomas, and Bartholomew Legate, two of whom are burned for heresy.

The essence of the Seeker position was a belief that the powers and authority granted to the apostles in the New Testament had been so corrupted and destroyed by the Church of Rome that no true church could be constituted until God had raised up a new race of apostles. As early as 1590 Henry Barrow had felt it necessary to counter the opinion that 'all extraordinary offices [in the church] have ceased, and so must all the building of Christ's church and the work of the ministry cease, until some second John the Baptist, or new apostles, be sent us down from heaven'.

Such views were attributed by the renegade Baptist Edmund Jessop to three brothers by name of Legate who lived – one can hardly say flourished – at the turn of the sixteenth and seventeenth centuries. All three met with unfortunate ends: Walter Legate was drowned 'while washing himself in a river' in the early seventeenth century; Thomas, who may at one time have been a member of Barrow's church, died in Newgate [prison] around 1607, where he had been confined for holding Arian views; and Bartholomew was burned at the stake at Smithfield for the same heresy in 1612. [35]

Our first curious parallel, then, between real-world Seekers and Ms. Rowling's world of wizards, beyond the many Florentine hermetic touches in every Potter novel, is a curious echo in the origins. Harry and Voldemort's first known ancestors are the three Peverell brothers, two of whom die horrible deaths consequent to their arrogance. The Seekers come to

[35]   Michael Watts, *The Dissenters: Volume I: From the Reformation to the French Revolution*, Oxford University Press, New York, 1986; pp
185

England via three brothers, two of whom are executed brutally by the state because of their outspoken heresy.

The rise of the Spiritual Seekers has a more specific Potter parallel in the person of John Everard, their most prolific exponent. And it has to be noted here that the Seekers were a real force to contend with by mid-century:

> According to Jessop, John Wilkinson, the Separatist leader in Colchester, also shared their opinions. But it was not until the ecclesiastical and social turmoil of the 1640's that the view gained wide acceptance 'that there must be new apostles before there could be a true constituted church'. 'The Sect of Seekers,' reported Thomas Edwards in 1646, 'grows very much, and all sorts of sectaries turn Seekers; many leave the congregations of Independents [and] Anabaptists, and fall to be Seekers, and not only people, but ministers also'.
> 'Very many of the Anabaptists are now turned Seekers', agreed Robert Baillie, including the future Ranter Lawrence Clarkson and the founder of Rhode Island, Roger Williams. They met together, explained William Penn, 'not formally to pray or preach..., but waited together in silence, and as anything arose in any one of their minds, that they thought savored of a divine spring, so they sometimes spoke'. [36]

Seekerism began to flourish during the ecclesiastical and spiritual turmoil of the 1640s and expanded rapidly during the Civil Wars (1642-48) in the northern counties of Yorkshire, Westmoreland, and Lancashire, and in the west in Bristol and even London. It reached its peak

---

36   *Michael Watts, op.cit; pp 185-186*

in the English Commonwealth under Oliver Cromwell, who remained uncommitted to any particular sect but exhibited some Seeker sympathy. The Seeker sect grew to such proportions that by 1646 army chaplain John Saltmarsh apparently considered it the fourth most important sect in England. Presbyterian Thomas Edwards feared that he would see all other sects "swallowed up in the Seekers."[37]

Seekerism as a religious movement only begins to grow during the chaos of the Civil War because of the translations and preaching of a Cambridge scholar named John Everard. He translates the German radical reformers and Ficino's work on alchemy as well – and preaches an anti-nomian, perfectionist seeker doctrine of spiritual alchemy.

The works of other Continental Spiritualists and occultists – Weigel, Agrippa, Niclaes, Franck, Eckhart – also made their way into English print in these years. Many of these were translations made by **John Everard** (1582? – 1641?), an Anglican minister in London who turned to Spiritualism in the 1620s. Reaching further back, Everard translated the central text of the hermetic tradition, the "Divine Pimander" of Hermes Trismegistus, which was published in 1650, nine years after his death. ...

Everard was a leading figure among a broad group called **the Seekers**, individuals who hoped for a new dispensation, the coming of the New Jerusalem. Never organized, except in occasional meetings of like minded persons, the Seekers collectively shaped many of the major doctrines of the sects that followed. Everard, with Giles

---

37   *Dan Vogel, Religious Seekers and the Advent of Mormonism, Signature Books, Salt Lake City, 1988; p 9.*

Randall and John Portage, can be seen as a bridge linking the Familist movement and Continental mysticism to the Seekers and the revolutionary sects. Early in the 1640s Randall and Portage preached the Familist ideas of a new dispensation and human deification, with a new emphasis on hermetic themes drawn from Boehme and other Continental sources. Randall argued that the indwelling of the Holy Ghost would allow a person to gain universal knowledge. Less concerned with the prospect of a literal New Jerusalem, Everard preached a mystical individualism informed by Familist doctrines of divinization and by a deep immersion in alchemical hermeticism.[38]

Even during the reign of Elizabeth the ideas of the radical reformers were already drifting across the channel into England. During the reign of James I (1603-25), **John Everard,** a Cambridge scholar who preached a curious blend of Seekerism and spiritual alchemy, translated into English selected works of Denck, Frank, and Castellio. It was during the period of Everard's preaching that Seekerism as a movement was born in England. 39

I'm hoping the name 'Everard' rings a bell with you. Review this scene from Chapter 22 of Order of the Phoenix if it doesn't -- Harry is reporting his "I attacked Mr. Weasley" vision to the Headmaster:

---

[38]   John Brooke, *The Refiner's Fire: The Making of Mormon Cosmology, 1644-1844, Cambridge University Press*, New York: 1994; pp 10, 22

[39]   *Dan Vogel, Religious Seekers and the Advent of Mormonism, Signature Books, Salt Lake City, 1988; p 9.*

But Dumbledore stood up so quickly that Harry jumped, and addressed one of the old portraits hanging very near the ceiling.

"Everard?" he said sharply. "And you too, Dilys!"

A sallow-faced wizard with short, black bangs and an elderly witch with long silver ringlets in the frame beside him, both of whom seemed to have been in the deepest of sleeps, opened their eyes immediately.

"You were listening?" said Dumbledore.

The wizard nodded, the witch said, "Naturally."

"The man has red hair and glasses," said Dumbledore. "Everard, you will need to raise the alarm, make sure he is found by the right people —"

Both nodded and moved sideways out of their frames, but instead of emerging in neighboring pictures (as usually happened at Hogwarts), neither reappeared; one frame now contained nothing but a backdrop of dark curtain, the other a handsome leather armchair. Harry noticed that many of the other headmasters and mistresses on the walls, though snoring and drooling most convincingly, kept sneaking peeks at him under their eyelids, and he suddenly understood who had been talking when they had knocked.

"Everard and Dilys were two of Hogwarts's most celebrated Heads," Dumbledore said, now sweeping around Harry, Ron, and Professor McGonagall and approaching the magnificent sleeping bird on his perch beside the door. "Their renown is such that both have portraits hanging in other important Wizarding institutions. As they are free to move between their own portraits they can tell us what may be happening elsewhere...."

Dumbledore replaced the instrument upon its spindly little table; Harry saw many of the old headmasters in the portraits follow him with their eyes, then, realizing that Harry was watching them, hastily pretend to be sleeping again. Harry wanted to ask what the strange silver instrument was for, but before he could do so, there was a shout from the top of the wall to their right; the wizard called Everard had reappeared in his portrait, panting slightly.

"Dumbledore!"

"What news?" said Dumbledore at once.

"I yelled until someone came running," said the wizard, who was mopping his brow on the curtain behind him, "said I'd heard something moving downstairs – they weren't sure whether to believe me but went down to check – you know there are no portraits down there to watch from. Anyway, they carried him up a few minutes later. He doesn't look good, he's covered in blood, I ran along to Elfrida Cragg's portrait to get a good view as they left -"

"Good," said Dumbledore as Ron made a convulsive movement, "I take it Dilys will have seen him arrive, then -"

You may think the name 'Everard' is a bit of a stretch to be making any kind of link between the beloved Headmaster Everard Proudfoot whose paintings are everywhere in the Wizarding World and the Seeker-Hermeticist John Everard of the 17th Century. There are three notes in this *Phoenix* Headmaster's Office scene that make me think it's actually quite a good link.

The first is that it *is* a very unusual name and the second is that Rowling gives it special emphasis in the one scene in the books where Albus Dumbledore works hermetic magic of spirit discernment (and ar-

190   *Harry Potter Smart Talk*

rives at the Christian formula of one person with two natures about Harry, the Christ figure). See *How Harry Cast His Spell's* chapter on *Order of the Phoenix* for that discussion in full.

The more obvious link, though, between Ms. Rowling's Everard Proudfoot and John Everard, Seeker and Christian Hermeticist, is his hair cut.

He's a 'Roundhead.' Everard's "short, black bangs" are the signature haircut of 17th Century radical Protestants. I think we have a match.

So, three brothers at the origin, Everard the Roundhead hermeticist at the peak, what is the Potter parallel with the Spiritual Seekers at their decline? In a word, 'Muggles.'

Meet the Muggletonians

There has been quite the bit of speculation about whence and why Ms. Rowling chose the word 'Muggles' as the preferred term of derision that magical folk use for people like Vernon and Petunia Dursley. Why this odd word to describe the great mass of humanity "without a drop of magic in 'em" and who are delighted to be "perfectly normal, thank you very much"?

I surveyed the speculative field at HogwartsProfessor. com[40] and found links to America slang for a doped cigarette, a record by Louis Armstrong, and the infamous Rah and the Muggles lawsuit brought by Nancy Stouffer. The most common assertion, albeit one made without any explanation other than the consonance of the words, was that 'Muggles' the word was

---

40   http://www.hogwartsprofessor.com/muggletonians-whence-potterverses-muggles/

somehow derived from the followers of one Lodowick Muggleton, the 'Muggletonians.'

As I hope you've guessed by now, the link is a lot stronger than a similar sound. The Muggletonians were a group of literal Seekers, who two hundred years before Joseph Smith, Jr., claimed to have found a new revelation, proclaimed their own. John Brooke, historian of the roots of Mormonism in the Seeker movements, describes the beliefs of these Muggles:

> The frustrated activism of the Fifth Monarchists was one response to the reversal of the tide of revolution in the early 1650's; the mystical quietism of the Muggggletonians and the Quakers was another. Accommodating their doctrine to the force of civil authority in Protectorate and Restoration, the Muggletonians and Quakers, with the Fifth Monarchists-turned-Sabbatarians, would be the only organized survivors of revolutionary radicalism. If the Quakers were to be distinguished by their numbers and by their reach into the American colonies, the Muggletonians were distinguished by their extreme interpretation of the hermetic-Joachimite tradition.
>
> Most fundamentally, the Muggletonians believed in a new dispensation. Rather than a future prospect, it had already arrived: a "Commission of the Spirit" had been revealed to two London tailors, John Reeves and Lodowick Muggleton, in February 1652. They were the Two Last Witnesses of Revelation 11:3, given a revelation to announce the opening of Joachim's Third Age. Reeves's *A Divine Looking Glass* was the sacred text for the new dispensation.
>
> Opposing the militant advocacy of the coming Kingdom of the Fifth Monarchists, the Muggletonians shared a broad set of hermetic

doctrines with the Seekers, Winstanley, and the Ranters, though giving each a unique twist.

- They believed in a primal materialism: creation had come from the substance of God.
- But they rejected the hermetic pantheism of a pervasive divinity: their God was a finite being about "five foot high," complete with bodily parts.
- Where other sects preached a universal salvation or divinization, the Muggletonians were predestinarian; the touchstone of election was belief in Muggletonian doctrine.

Here they introduced a theme developed by Winstanley and rooted in Boehme's hermeticism, that of the "two seeds." Good and evil forces rested in the sexual events of Genesis: the good seed of the "blessed Israelites" was the product of the union of Adam and Eve, and the bad seed of the "cursed Canaanites" was the product of Eve's seduction by the devil. Descending among the separate peoples of Adam and Cain, the two seeds had been mixed by the intermarriage of these two lineages, and caused good and evil behavior in humanity.

But rather than elevating reason, as Winstanley did, Muggletonian belief made it the mark of the devil's seed, with faith the mark of Adam's seed. Belief in Muggletonian prophecy was a sufficient sign of a preponderance of Adams' seed, and thus election. Organized among a loose group of small merchants and artisans in the Midlands and the south of England, Muggletonianism survived in a small way into the twentieth century. It would have interesting echoes among the sectarians of eighteenth-century southeast Connecticut, the region from which Joseph Smith's mother came, and in the texts and ethos of the Mormon church.[41]

Prof. Brooke makes three connections between Muggletonians and Mormons, namely, (1) the "two seeds" doctrine being reflected in the *Book of Mormons'* Nephites and Lamanites, (2) the finite, strictly anthropomorphic God the Father, and (3) their determined efforts "to establish and maintain a firm boundary between their theology and the story of occult influences deeply embedded in their early history" (*Fire*, pages 28-29).

All very interesting, but it doesn't tell us anything about the Dursleys, does it?

Today it must seem a reach because the Muggletonians as radical non-conformists hardly seem more than a coincidental assonance with Harry's Muggle Aunt and Uncle, radical conformists. Note, however, that the Muggletonians are spiritual materialists suggestive of the materialism-in-lieu-of-spirituality of the Dursleys, they are both anti-rationalists, if again, for very different reasons (sic), and they are pre-destinarian. Harry's blood lines doom him, if the Dursleys will struggle to squeeze the magic out of him. There's more to the word 'Muggle — a Muggletonian link! — than Nancy Stouffer dreamed.

To grasp the reason why Ms. Rowling's wizards despise Muggletonians requires two links, namely, the Seekers with the Quakers and the Quakers relations with the Muggletonians.

---

41   *John Brooke, The Refiner's Fire: The Making of Mormon Cosmology, 1644-1844, Cambridge University Press, New York: 1994; pp 24-25*

As we noted, the radical non-conformist sects after the Restoration and Glorious Revolution are persecuted and all but legislated out of existence by the Five Mile Act and others. The Spiritual Seekers with their border-line occult beliefs, not too surprisingly, find cover under the almost hermetic 'inner light' doctrines of the Society of Friends or 'Quakers.'

Remember the Spiritual Seekers are looking for an *inner* Second Coming:

> 'Though I speak sometimes unto men in the flesh,' wrote William Ebery in 1652, 'yet my spirit is silent unto God; thus I am wholly silent, waiting as one of the dry bones in the dust, when the Lord will raise me with all his people out of our graves, by revealing his glory in us.' The gatherings of the Seekers in the early 1650's, like the meetings of the Fifth Monarchists, were marked by a sense of expectation, but expectations very different from those entertained by the millenarians. It was not 'a glory without' for which Erbery waited 'but a glory to be *revealed in us*, and that in this life.'[42]

This inner revelation, shorn of much of the hermetic perfectionism of Everard, is key to the Quaker beliefs about the 'inner light.' The Spiritual Seekers, in the crucible of state persecution at the end of the 17th Century, find a home within George Fox's Society of Friends.

The Quakers inherited the world of the radical sects. Beginning in the north of England in 1652,

42   *Michael Watts, op.cit.; pp 185-186*

by 1660 they had gathered perhaps 40,000 people into their meetings. Quakerism became the refuge of many – perhaps most – of those who, during the revolutionary years, had seen the possibility of a religion of equals, universally saved by their recognition of a pervasive, internalized divinity.

The sum of Quakerism lies in the **Inner Light**, the presence of the divine in the human soul. This inner divinity was "the coming of Christ in the spirit to save his people from sin": it was an internalized millennium, a new dispensation superseding all church ordinances and sacred texts. The revelations, or "openings," that came to George Fox in 1647 provided the central inspiration for Quakerism, but the evidence suggests to many historians that Familist doctrines of divinization and Jacob Boehme's and **John Everard's** writings were important in shaping the ground for both Fox's vision and the reception of his message.

The very dimensions of early Quakerism and its antiauthoritarian strain meant that diverse interpretations and influences were at work. If the coming of the Inner Light brought an internal millennium, James Nayler in 1656 acted it out in a very external way, riding into Bristol dressed as Christ and with a following of worshiping women. One Quaker went so far as to claim to be "above St. Peter & equal with God." George Fox himself may have hoped that he could achieve perfection and a hermetic "unity with the creation."

He was reputed to have worked as many as one hundred and fifty miracle healings of lunatics and exorcisms of the bewitched. His healing powers rested in his claim of having been "renewed into the image of God by Christ Jesus, to the state of Adam, which he was in before he fell," exactly the aspiration of **the hermetic *magus***. And the very name of "Quaker" derived from the tremors and shaking that ran through the early meetings, "outward manifestations of the inward workings of the power of God." The radical sects, in sum, briefly realized the promise of divine perfection and of an optimistic participation in the cosmos, synthesized in the Renaissance figure of the **Christian-hermetic *magus***.[43] *(highlighting mine)*

Ms. Rowling's witches and wizards are the fictional, underground survivors of the real-world Everard-ian "Christian hermetic magi." The end of the 17th Century with its post Restoration and Glorious Revolution persecutions of nonconformist sects sees the assimilation of the Everard Seekers into the Quaker movement of George Fox. George Fox dies in 1691 and the Quakers begin their determined efforts "to establish and maintain a firm boundary between their theology and the story of occult influences deeply embedded in their early history."[44] 1692, consequently, is the date Ms. Rowling's witches and wizards go underground.

But what's the friction with the Muggles about?

"Inner Light" *Logos* soteriology is dicey enough, frankly; its roots in Florentine cabalistic alchemy and Eastern Christian traditions aren't sufficiently Politically or *Theologically* Correct for the Ministry of the time, The Glorious Revolution's Church of England. Everard's hermetic Spiritual Seekers, then, are assimilated into the 'inner light' non-conformist beliefs of George Fox and the Quakers. These Spiritual Seekers, however, don't get along well with the proto-Mormons, the Literal Seekers called Muggletonians.

---

43   John Brooke, op.cit; p 25
44   Brooke, op.cit, p 29

In fact, the Agonist claims in 'Harry Potter and the War Against the Muggles' that

> In contrast to Cromwell, who wanted to tolerate all shades of English Protestant opinion, the Muggletonians were ferociously intolerant, and in fact famous for successfully wishing the death of several of their peace-loving opponents, the Quakers.[45]

Ms. Rowling chooses the word "Muggles," then, to describe non-Magical people because the Muggletonians were the enemies and rivals of the Quaker/Seekers. She calls the key player on the Quidditch pitch a "Seeker" and her hero a "natural Seeker" because her Witches and Wizards are the non-conformist **Christian-hermetic *magi*** of the Radical Reformation who went underground at the end of the 17th Century. The International Statute of Wizarding Secrecy, again, the defining piece of legislation that sets out the way of life parameters for Magical Folk everywhere, is written and passed in 1692.

Review of What We've Learned Today

Head Spinning? Mine, too. Let's go over this one more time:

The "Spiritualist Seekers" who were perfectionists as well as radical primitivists and non-conformists disappear into the Quaker movement of George Fox. These pious pacifist Friends, however, during the persecutions of Charles II, James II, and William II, shed in large part the magical, hermetic, even occult beliefs of the Italian Renaissance. In brief, the Christian hermetic Magi of John Everard vanish into history.

---

45   *http://agonist.org/mmeo/20080330/harry_potter_and_the_war_against_muggles*

So what? Well, we have a bunch of Harry Potter connections here that point to a historical connection between these magical Christian Seekers and the wizarding world that went underground in 1692.

The Three Legate brothers, two of whom die horrible deaths, bring the Seeker faith to England and have their shadow in the 'Tale of the Three Brothers' in *Beedle the Bard*, the story of Harry Potter and Voldemort's ancestors and of the Deathly Hallows.

John Everard is the heart and engine of English Seekerism and we meet him – complete with Roundhead haircut in Dumbledore's office in Chapter 22 of *Order of the Phoenix*. Dumbledore dispatches Everard, whom he calls one of "Hogwarts most celebrated heads" to find Mr. Weasley at the Ministry.

Seekers, of course, are mentioned by name in every Quidditch match. They are the star players who fly above the conflict of contrary teams in search of the Golden Snitch, which flying gold ball is a symbol used in alchemical texts for the Philosopher's Stone. When the Seeker achieves this perfection, the game is over, no matter the score of the game going on below.

We have, too, all the references to Florence and the hermetic arts, none of which are used fatalistically as Calvinists might; Firenze's astrology and Dumbledore's snake divination are sciences for gaining information for choices to be made.

Did I mention Chocolate Frog Cards for Agrippa and Paracelsus?

And we have the Muggles; the only enemy that the Quakers had among radical non-conformists, curiously enough, during the Age of Persecution, were the Muggletonian sect who denied the existence of a church like our Seekers but who also thought human perfection was impossible – no magic or divinization.

Conclusion: William Penn's Deathly Hallows Epigraph and 1692

Let's look at the 3 questions I said I wanted to answer today:

- Why 1692 for the International Statute of Wizarding Secrecy?
- What does this date tell us about wizards, especially those in the UK?
- Does this information help us understand HP more meaningfully?

From the top, then! *Why 1692?*

1692 is the date of the Salem witch Trials and the death of George Fox, the leader of the Quakers whose miraculous healings distinguished the early movement. As reflected in the Puritan attack on "magical" Christians – witches! -- in Plymouth and the Spiritual Seekers led by Roger Sherman in Rhode island, it was a time of great persecution of Seekers in the UK.

Ms. Rowling chooses 1692, then, not arbitrarily or accidentally, but deliberately, because she has an important point to make through this date. She has a left a trail of transparencies leading to the same meaning: think of Florence/Firenze, the Dante scenes ("Look – at --me!"), Frog Cards, Alchemy, Astrology, Memory Magic, symbols of Christ and the Resurrection, Seekers in Quidditch, Nicolas Flamel, John Everard, The Three Brothers, and the Muggletonian–like—Muggles.

The date and these pointers all tell us that the wizards and witches of her story are the descendants of the Spiritual Seekers, Christian hermetic magi who survived through the centuries under the Invisibility Cloak of the International Statute of Wizarding Secrecy. They disappeared when the radical, Spiritual Seekers disappeared *because they are the same group.*

What does this date tell us about wizards, especially those in the UK?

What this tells us about UK witches and wizards is that they are Christians, for one, thing, but Christians pursuing perfection in Christ outside of any Church or exterior ritual. Theirs is an interior perfection of the inner light and heart. Ms. Rowling's magical people are radical non-conformists and Seekers of the greater life in Christ.

Does this help us to understand Harry Potter more meaningfully?

I think so. Ms. Rowling chose a passage from Penn's *Fruits of Solitude* (1693/1702) as one of the epigraphs for *Deathly Hallows* and said in an interview that these epigraphs "just say it all to me they really do."

> "I'd known if was going to be those two passages since *Chamber* was published. I always knew if I could use them at the beginning of book seven that I'd ...up the ending perfectly. If they were relevant, then I went where I needed to go."[46]

William Penn, of course, is the world's most famous Quaker, and his epigraph reflects the hermetic teachings of the radical Seekers about the conjunction and immortality of believers, "Friends," in the mirror of

46   *MTV News.com, Harry Potter' Author J.K. Rowling Opens Up About Books' Christian Imagery, Shawn Adler, Oct 17 2007; http://www.mtv. com/news/articles/1572107/20071017/story.jhtml*

God's Word or Logos. Ms. Rowling has said "the key" to understanding her work is Harry and Dumbledore's last words to one another in the 'King's Cross scene in *Deathly Hallows*, words she said she "waited seventeen years to write."[47] I explain that passage in *Deathly Hallows Lectures* chapter 5, 'The Seeing Eye,' and in *Hog's Head Conversations*, chapter 3, 'The Deathly Hallows Epigraphs.'

Both "the key" passage to understanding Harry Potter and the *Deathly Hallows* epigraphs, it turns out, are about the Word or *Logos* of God as the origin of reality and knowledge, an origin we recognize and know in love. I doubt it will surprise you to learn that this is a core belief of the Florentine Renaissance perfectionists and of Christian high fantasy writers in the United Kingdom after Coleridge.

Here is what I hope you take away from this talk.

First, this is, of course, entirely speculative and I suspect my necessarily brief theological and historical surveys have experts in the field groaning. I do hope, though, that you thought it was fun and that the possibility Ms. Rowling's wizarding world has a real world counter-part is an intriguing one. I certainly enjoyed following those textual clues to their historical referents.

---

47   "Ser invisible... eso sería lo más," *El Pais*, Juan Cruz, 8 Feb 2008
Q: There's this dialogue between Harry and Professor Dumbledore: "Is this real? Or has this been happening inside my head?"
A: And Dumbledore says: "Of course it is happening inside your head, but why on earth would that mean that is not real?" That dialogue is the key; I've waited seventeen years to use those lines. Yes, that's right. All this time I've worked to be able to write those two phrases; writing Harry entering the forest and Harry having that dialog.
http://www.the-leaky-cauldron.org/2008/2/9/jkr-discusses-dursley-family-religion-us-presidential-election-and-more-in-new-interview

Next, I hope that you see that this revelation of why wizards went underground in 1692 (and why Wizards and Muggles aren't friendly!) makes Christian objections to Harry Potter, the so-called Potter-Panic of the Harry Haters, that much more ironic. Not only are the witches and wizards *Christian*, but, because the historical Spiritual Seekers of John Everard – our witches and wizards – were driven underground by other Christians, it seems fitting somehow that the descendents of Seeker persecutors would attack Harry and company as well.

Thank you for your kind attention today, for listening to the Potter Pundits at The Leaky Cauldron's PotterCasts, and, in advance, for writing me at john@ HogwartsProfessor.com to continue this conversation.

CPSIA information can be obtained at www.ICGtesting.com
Printed in the USA
BVOW011234141211

278339BV00003B/77/P

9 780982 963302